BETTER LOVE NOW!

BETTER LOVE NOW!

MAKING YOUR MARRIAGE A LIFELONG LOVE AFFAIR

TOMMY NELSON with DAVID DELK

Nashville, Tennessee

ISBN: 978-0-8054-4072-0

Published by B & H Publishing Group,
Nashville, Tennessee

Dewey Decimal Classification: 306.81
Subject Heading: MARRIAGE \ LOVE

08 09 10 11 12 15 14 13 12 11 10 9 8 7 6 5 4 3 2 1

To my beloved wife of thirty-two years, Teresa.

You have followed, labored, delighted, honored, and embraced the vision of an oft-times-stumbling and all-too-mannish husband.

Contents

Acknowledgments

To Doug Hudson, who has constantly seen the vision of what can be.

To the leadership of LifeWay and their commitment to co-labor with dreamers.

To David Delk and his skill in the deft arrangement of ideas.

To the saints and faithful brethren of Saint Simons Island Community Church at Saint Simons Island, Georgia, who first heard the teaching that became this book.

Introduction

HOW CAN YOU HAVE better love now? Let's start by understanding the condition of marriage today.

To do that, imagine yourself having a conversation with my father forty years ago.

You ask him, "Do you lie, cheat, or steal?"

He says, "No."

You ask, "Why not?"

He says, "Because you are not supposed to."

You say, "Why not?"

He says, "Because it is wrong."

You decide to push it a little bit. "Says who?"

He starts to get a little irritated and says, "God."

You challenge him, saying, "Explain who God is."

At that point my father probably would have looked at you funny. He may not have been able to give you an analytical treatise on theology proper. But he would have had an instinctive idea through the culture he was raised in about an infinite, personal God. He grew up knowing about a God who created man. This God gave man his dignity. This God gave man a conscience, so he would know right from wrong. My dad knew that this instinctive knowledge of God was amplified and clarified by the giving of his law and the incarnation of Jesus Christ.

Dad would have looked at you funny because he would have wondered why in the world you didn't know this too.

My father, his father, and his father before him would have had innate ideas about God, the order of creation, right and wrong, institutions, authority, leading, and following. Your father and his father and his father probably did too.

But we live in a different day than our parents, grandparents, and great-grandparents lived in. Something happened in about the mid-1900s—we punted the Judeo-Christian worldview. So people no longer default to seeing the world through a biblical perspective on truth and reality.

Now our worldview has become "a-theistic." Man is the standard of all right and wrong. Because man in himself is not absolute, he cannot serve as a consistent standard. And so morality has become an arbitrary thing.

What are the consequences? Those institutions that stand or fall upon the knowledge of a creator God who is infinite and personal are stumbling. Government, business, schools, households—all derive their stability from a recognition of authority, leadership, accountability, respect, and reverence. And all of them are suffering greatly. Our modern worldview has created a breakdown in all the institutions that depend on the existence of moral absolutes and submission to them.

You may be saying, "Thanks for the history lesson, Tommy, but what does this have to do with me?" Believe it or not, these changes have a lot to do with why you are reading this book: the institution that has suffered the most is marriage, and that includes yours.

Introduction

Look around your workplace and your neighborhood, and you will see the devastation left from the failure of marriages. There is an incredible hunger for information and teaching about marriage. You can't turn on the TV without seeing some talk show or news magazine special about marriage. The best-seller list always seems to have at least one book on relationships firmly entrenched near the top.

In my ministry I have taught and written several times on romance and marriage from the Song of Solomon. Every time I teach this material, my audience doubles. I taught it at my church in the early 1990s, and we almost doubled. I taught it for singles at the Metro Bible Study in Dallas, and we went from 1,200 to 2,000 in a few weeks. I taught it again at Metro a few years later, and we went from 2,000 to 4,000.

I think I'm pretty good on Romans, but my audience doesn't double when I teach on that book. What's the difference? People know there is something wrong with our culture's understanding of marriage.

Without a foundation of belief in God, we are cut loose from the mother ship. When an astronaut goes on a space walk, he makes sure he is securely tethered to the ship. If that tether is somehow cut, the astronaut could get sucked right out into space.

If man is not tethered to God and his revelation of himself in the Bible, then man's not sure who he is, who you are, what government is, what morality is, what marriage is, what being a husband means, what being a wife means, and on and on. Without God, people get sucked out into space. The machine of the cosmos just eats you up when you think you are nothing more than just another insignificant, accidental part of it.

This worldview has infiltrated the church with terrible results. Marriage is no longer an apologetic for the faith. When I first started in the ministry, you could point to the lack of divorce among Christians as a reason that someone should trust Christ. Not anymore. Divorce is just as prevalent inside the church as outside.

I wrote this book to bring folks back to a biblical worldview concerning marriage. But you need to know that this is not Tommy Nelson's best ideas about marriage. A book like that wouldn't be worth the paper it was printed on. Everybody's got an opinion on marriage today—go to any bookstore, and you will find hundreds of books on the topic. It doesn't really matter what people think; it matters what God says.

That's why we are going to look carefully at what the Bible says about marriage. Build your marriage on God's revelation and it will never fail.

This book is also unique because we will come at this biblical teaching from an interesting angle. We are going to take a look at six major areas of your marriage, consider what the Bible says, then look at the expectations and assumptions that a husband and wife bring into marriage for each area. We all have dreams and hopes and fears that color our perspective and experiences. If your mate is not holding up their end of the bargain, you are going to be disappointed. And if you aren't doing your part, then you are going to have a frustrated spouse.

This book will help you get to the place in your marriage where you've always wanted to be. It will help you find better love now. Marriage can be a lifelong honeymoon—when you follow the guidebook and live by the principles of God's Word.

Finally, I wrote this book because I know bad marriages—we've had a lot of good ones in our church, but we've also had our share of bad ones. And I've been right in the trenches with more husbands and wives than I could count. Frankly, I'd rather you read this book and let God fix you now, than see you in my office five years from now with a box of Kleenex. God has something more for you than a mediocre marriage. My prayer is that he would use this book to get you to the place where your marriage reflects the glory, harmony, and love within the three persons of God himself. That's what he's made you for, and that's what will satisfy your soul.

Fence Posts

I know, I know. My wife has already told me. It's pretty strange to start a book about having a better marriage with a picture of a fence—not exactly the most romantic thing in the world. It's also not an everyday object that most suburban twenty-somethings are dealing with.

But that's OK because I wrote this book and I'm from Texas. In Texas, fences are important. In fact, it's impossible to have a ranch without a fence. Fences define the boundaries, keep predators out, and keep livestock in.

If you've ever had to work with fences, you quickly learned that a fence is only as good as its posts. Even in the suburbs, that

backyard fence will fall down or blow over when the fence posts begin to rot.

One thing I know about fences from trial and error: you can't tell how sturdy a fence post is by looking at it from above ground. Long before you see any evidence of a problem, the post may be rotting under the damp, dark earth.

That's why farmers used to look for heartwood to use for fence posts. This is wood found in the center of the tree. Sapwood near the bark turns into heartwood as a tree grows. During the growth, certain compounds are deposited in the heartwood that make it resistant to disease and insects. These same chemicals make heartwood fence posts last underground.

Marriage can often be like a fence post. Long before there are any visible signs of wear and tear above ground, the foundation of a relationship can be rotting away. That's why we need to make sure our marriages are made of heartwood—that they have the essential components to remain strong amid the stress and strain of modern life.

This book will help you look at six "fence posts" in your marriage that need to be maintained to have better love now. Keep these six areas strong, and your marriage will last a lifetime.

We will cover the six areas in three steps:

- First, you will evaluate how you and your spouse are currently doing in an area. I'll give you a short, guided discussion you can use to make your communication effective. This should take you no more than fifteen minutes.
- Second, I'll give you two chapters of teaching to help you in an area of your marriage. The first chapter will help you gain a biblical understanding. The second chapter will dis-

cuss how this area applies to husbands and wives and our everyday lives.
- Finally, I'll give you some questions and application steps that you can use to make concrete improvement in each area. This will allow you to process what you've read and put it into practice.

My goal is not to write another marriage book. There are plenty of nice ones out there. I'm writing this to give you the chance to actually change your life and your marriage.

Marriage is God's first institution and helps you reflect his image in relationship to your life partner. I don't know how the stakes could be any higher than that. That's why my earnest prayer is that God would use this book to help you have better love now.

Fence Post 1: Priorities

One of the keys to having better love now is to make sure that you treat the most important things as the most important things. Our priorities determine how we invest our time and energy. What do your schedule and calendar say about your priorities? What about your checkbook? What are you working for and dreaming about?

When our priorities take us away from our spouses and families, we are being distracted from what is really important.

The next two chapters will help you reevaluate and align your priorities within marriage. But first, I'm going to give you a chance to have a short discussion to discover what you both think about the priorities of your marriage.

Six times in this book I'm going to ask you to rate your marriage—one for each of the six areas we are discussing. My goal is to get you thinking about each area before you read what I've written and what the Bible says. I'm also hoping you'll have a short, ten-minute discussion with your spouse to prepare you for what God might want to do in your heart.

Fence Post 1: Priorities

Wife's Perspective

How would you rate your marriage in the area of your priorities? Use the following to chart your thoughts.

With a pencil, draw a line on each fence post to show your rating for your marriage in the area of priorities.

Our priorities are just right.

Our priorities are really out of whack.

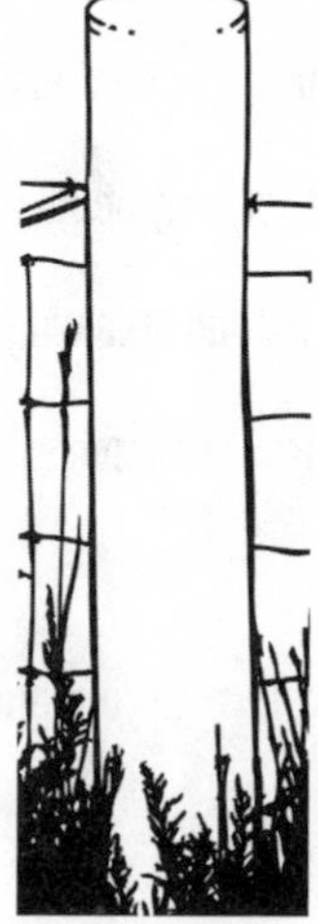

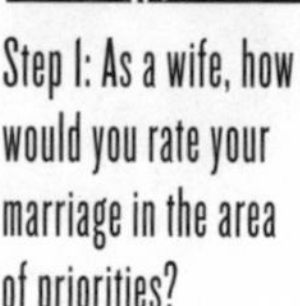

Step 1: As a wife, how would you rate your marriage in the area of priorities?

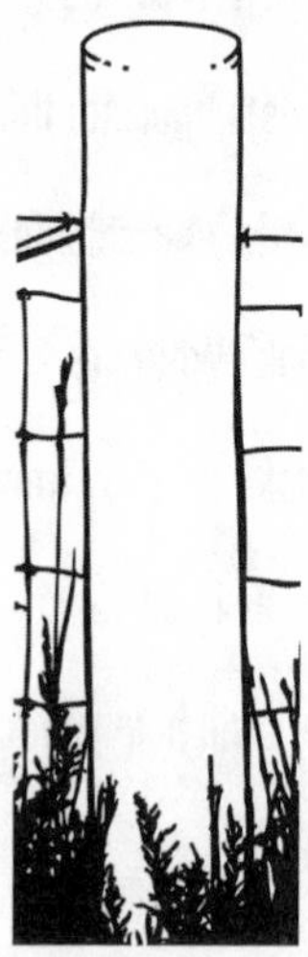

Step 2: How will your husband rate your marriage in the area of priorities?

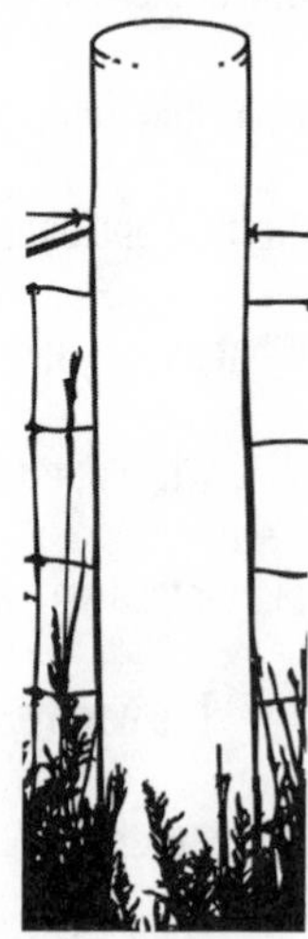

Step 3: What will your husband say you thought? Mark where he will say you rated your marriage in the area of priorities.

Fence Post 1: Priorities

Husband's Perspective

As a husband, how would you rate your marriage in the area of your priorities? Use the following to chart your thoughts.

With a pencil, draw a line on each fence post to show your rating in the area of priorities.

Our priorities are just right.

Our priorities are really out of whack.

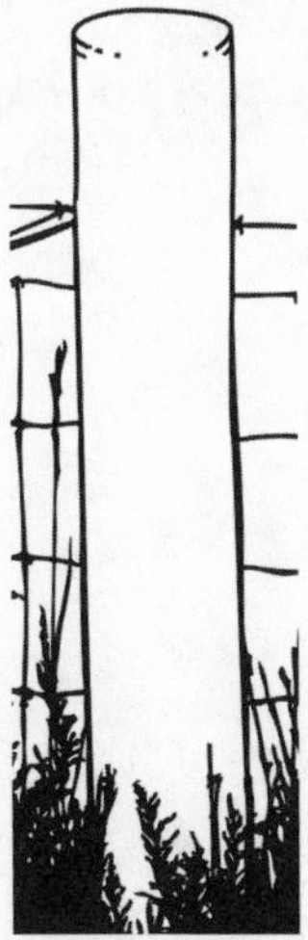

Step 1: As a husband, how would you rate your marriage in the area of priorities?

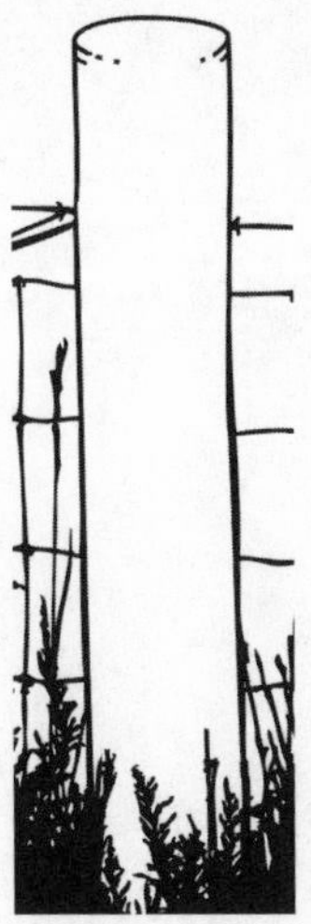

Step 2: How will your wife rate your marriage in the area of priorities?

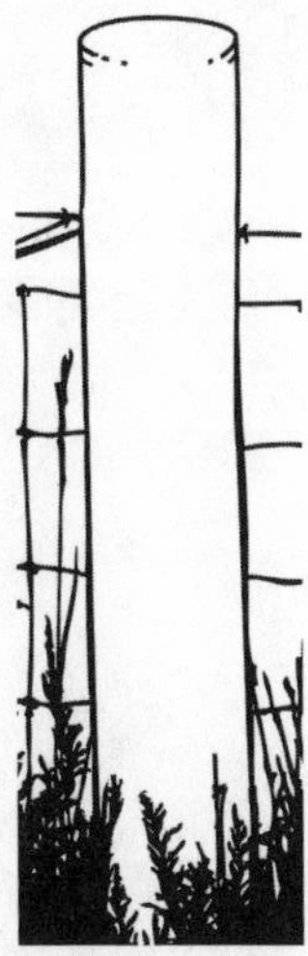

Step 3: What will your wife say you thought? Mark where she will say that you rated your marriage in the area of priorities.

For Discussion:

Take about ten minutes and work your way from step 1 to step 3. For each step, share why you rated your priorities the way you did. (Note that the wife's step 3 corresponds to the husband's step 2.)

What issues does this raise that you want to consider more deeply? Are there areas in which you and your spouse have a different perspective? Have you seen some potential areas of conflict that need to be addressed?

Have a short prayer, asking God to help you both change in any ways necessary to have better love now.

Now read the chapters and talk through the discussion and application questions at the end.

Chapter I

Your Priorities and Your Marriage

Recently, I spoke to a good friend of mine who attends another church in our city. He shared about two different couples in his church, both in their early forties with two or three kids. Both couples announced in the last month that they are splitting up. You probably know some couples like this as well.

Having been a pastor for more than thirty years, I've seen my share of couples whose marriages end up lifeless and cold. The remarkable thing is that in the vast majority of cases, their situations are not all that complicated. A husband and wife will sit in my office and say that after ten years of marriage, they don't know how to make it work. And yet, as we talk, invariably it comes down to things they've known since they were small children. It may take an hour to get to it, but in the end, I find that someone is not being kind to their spouse—not listening, not paying attention, or not being respectful. It's always the little things, and it's really not that complicated.

The destruction of a marriage doesn't happen quickly. If it did, more couples might see it coming and do something about it. Unfortunately, it decays over a long period of time, like the fence posts. Month to month, it doesn't seem like there is much difference, but over a period of years, the heart rots out.

The truth is that a godly marriage is built on simple things and is destroyed by simple things. When a marriage goes south, it's because one or both spouses misplaced their priorities. They began to think something else was more important than their spouse. Over time their friends, their children, their jobs, their hobbies—something—began to take the most special place in their heart. And their spouse was pushed aside.

Fred and Brenda were living the American dream. They were involved in a campus ministry in college, got married shortly after graduation, and joined a church when they graduated. They looked like the perfect couple.

Fred started his career with a bang. Soon they were expecting their first child. Then their second. Fred got a couple of promotions and got busier and busier at work. Pretty soon he didn't have time to spend with God every day. Church became more of a superficial commitment that they did because they were supposed to. Fred began to value all the things his work was providing; Brenda valued their home and their children. Their relationship became more and more shallow. Their physical intimacy dried up. He became angry; she became defensive. Alienation and loneliness began to creep in. Then a third party came along and Fred had an affair. Their marriage lay in ruins.

It wasn't one big choice that led to this destruction. It was living with misplaced priorities over a period of years. They didn't know their marriage was having its heart eaten out. From the outside looking in, you would think Fred and Brenda had it all. But beneath the surface, their wrong priorities led to the deterioration of their relationship. They didn't keep their fence posts strong.

The way to avoid this in your marriage is to start having better love now. Marriages don't stand still; they either get better or they get worse. Think back over the last weeks and months. In which direction is your marriage heading?

How do you make sure your marriage is heading in the right direction on a consistent basis? The first step is to keep your priorities straight. Your priorities will determine the choices and actions you take on an everyday basis.

I'm going to walk you through eight key priorities that ought to be a daily and weekly focus in your marriage. These are not optional ideas that might make a good marriage better. These are not "hangnail" issues that you can clip and bandage up so everything's fine.

If you don't get these areas right, your marriage won't be right. I'm not saying you won't be able to peacefully inhabit the same house with your spouse. Plenty of couples do that. I'm not saying you won't be able to look nice to your neighbors and friends at church. There are a lot of couples who go through the motions.

You can survive in your marriage without focusing on these priorities, but you will not experience a biblical marriage. Priorities determine whether your marriage is moving forward or moving backward. You must orient your heart and life correctly to have better love now.

So here, with a diagnostic scorecard for each one, are the eight biblical priorities that make the greatest difference in marriage.

1. Your Individual Time with God

The first priority for any couple in marriage is each person's individual time with God. As a husband or wife, your spiritual life is the fountain out of which everything else flows. Each person needs to spend time in the Word every day. You need to pray every day about the things that are important to you. You need to be quiet and listen for the Holy Spirit as you study God's Word.

If one of you gets out of a daily vibrant interaction with God, then you are just parroting what you think you should act like as a spouse. You are just mimicking what you have seen in other good couples. Basically, you are faking it. Faking it works OK when everything is going well, but when troubles come, faking it leads to disaster. Make it a priority to be in your Bible every day and spend time with God.

My wife and I made a vow before marrying to spend time with God every single day as individuals. God has been faithful to remind me often of that commitment. Both of us are still absolutely convinced of how important this is—it's made all the difference.

How would you say you are doing
on the priority of your daily time with God?
Poorly 1 2 3 4 5 Very Well

2. Your Friendship

Another priority for any couple needs to be their friendship. They have to work every day on being friends. They have to be careful how they speak to each other. They have to pay attention and be responsive.

There is always a low-grade fever in marriage. With two sinful human beings living in close proximity, it doesn't take much to let that fever become a raging infection. One of the most effective ways to keep it in check is to make your friendship a priority.

One of the staff members at our church affectionately calls his wife "milady." She will respond by calling him "m'lord." They found that this courtesy and tradition helps keep their friendship alive. What can you do on a regular basis to stimulate friendship in your marriage?

How would you rate your friendship with your spouse?

Strangers 1 2 3 4 5 Best Friends

3. Quality Time Together

In today's fast-paced culture, it's impossible to maintain a friendship and a marriage without making quality time a priority. Couples need to be diligent and creative in finding ways to withdraw together. Make time to talk and listen.

Short periods of concentrated time can work. Teresa and I love to take drives together (especially before gas went to three dollars a gallon). Have a date night. Take walks together. Go away for a night at a budget hotel. Just make sure that one of your highest priorities is to spend quality time with your spouse.

Joe and Lisa are good friends with Tom and Joan. They have developed a wonderful habit. They alternate having date nights on Saturday nights. The first week, Joe and Lisa will go out, and their kids will go to Tom and Joan's house to spend the night. They'll meet them at church on Sunday morning. The next week, Tom and Joan will go out on Saturday night and drop their kids off at Joe and Lisa's. Not only do they get to spend an evening alone without the kids; they also get to spend a morning together as well. What creative ways are you finding to spend quality time together?

How would you rate the amount of quality time you spend with your spouse?

Almost None 1 2 3 4 5 Just Right

4. Good Sex

Couples also need to make it a priority not just to have sex but to have good sex. When they have sex, they have to take the time to invest in each other. Sexuality is a gift from God. As a part of God's plan, it is quite literally "re-creation." If it's worth having sex as a couple, it's worth having good sex. (I'm going to go on to the next priority, but don't worry—this subject is so important that we are going to spend an entire chapter on it later in the book.)

How would you rate the sexual aspect of your marriage?

Not So Good 1 2 3 4 5 *Really Good Sex*

5. Direction for Your Marriage

Couples that last and thrive have the sense that they are headed somewhere. They know that they want to accomplish something as a couple and through their marriage. They believe that God has brought them together for ministry and to make a difference for his kingdom, not just to have a happy little suburban American home.

Of course I get paid to do ministry through my church, but Teresa and I would minister to others no matter what career I had chosen. Teresa loves to lead her small group and work with the international students at the university near our house.

I see this with other couples in our church. We have a coach in our church who is incredibly busy. His wife is wonderful and involved in a million ways in our church and community. Yet this couple makes sure that they have one night a week to help facilitate a discipleship study with other couples. They've made discipling other men and women a cornerstone of their relationship with one another. What is the larger vision that you and your spouse have given yourselves to?

How would you rate the direction of your marriage?

Sort of Aimless 1 2 3 4 5 *Going with God*

6. Your Children

An author on the family for more than forty years, Howard Hendricks once said that nothing can be worse for a marriage than building it on children, and nothing can be worse for children than building a marriage on them.

It may sound obvious, but I've seen a lot of couples get offtrack because they differed in how to make their children a priority. I've seen the kids become too much a priority for a mom or dad, taking over the life of the family. I've also seen a mom or dad disengage from the kids and leave the child-rearing to their partner. That won't work for long.

I knew a couple who were so affectionate that it was almost embarrassing to be with them in public. Within two years after their first child came, they were in counseling. The spouses had adjusted differently to the child, and one of them felt alienated. The child became the central focus of their marriage and their problems. Nothing could be worse.

Make your children a priority in your marriage. Don't make them the center of your marriage, but make time for them. Lead them to faith. Model your love for God and love for others. Show them what it means to be a Christian man and a Christian woman.

How well are you doing
at making your children a priority in your marriage?

Not So Good 1 2 3 4 5 *Just Right*

7. Humility

I know it's corny, but I still get caught up watching the 1950s mind-set of Ward and June Cleaver in *Leave It to Beaver.* They had such deference for one another. Ward looked out for June, and June looked out for Ward. Each considered the other as more important than themselves.

Successful couples have a stance of humility toward their spouse. The whole basis of marriage is based on humility—that you are more important than I am. Paul says, "be subject to one another in the fear of Christ" (Eph. 5:21). The only way to be submissive to other people is to consider them as more important than you—to humble yourself. "Do nothing from selfishness or empty conceit, but with humility of mind regard one another as more important than yourselves" (Phil. 2:3).

Are you self-oriented in your daily interactions with your spouse? Are you trying to preserve your conceit and pride? Love "does not seek its own" (1 Cor. 13:5). If you forget the priority of humility in your marriage, you are heading down a dangerous track. A stance of humility in marriage leads to better love now.

How well are you doing at humility?
(Yeah, I know this question seems ironic, but you can evaluate yourself without being proud, especially if you remember that Christ is the one who is changing your life.)
Way Too Proud 1 2 3 4 5 *Living in Humility*

8. Repentance

You've seen couples in which each person refuses to admit wrongdoing. If they have a spat in public, the best you can hope for is a negotiated settlement. One spouse will offer a "pseudo apology" with lots of "buts" that end up placing blame on the other person. The other will respond with silence and a look that says, "I'm big enough to keep loving you even though you are a jerk." A couple like this is heading for hard times unless they learn to truly repent.

Closely related to the priority of humility is the priority of repentance. Sinful men and sinful women are going to make mistakes. You are going to get offtrack. You are going to harm your spouse. You are going to do wrong to your kids.

The real question is, what are you going to do after you mess up? If you make repentance a priority, you will be willing to make it right. You'll want to fix it. You'll say to your spouse, "I'm gonna change what I have to change to make you happier." When you lose the priority of repentance, small problems become big problems, and you are headed for trouble.

How well are you doing at repentance?

Stiff-Necked 1 2 3 4 5 *Repenting Daily*

Well, how'd you do with your priorities? Wherever you are now, if you make the commitment to get things right in terms of your priorities, you will be well on your way to better love now.

Let's apply these ideas to the unique situations of men and women. When your spouse stood at the altar and heard you say, "I do," what exactly did they expect about your priorities?

Chapter 2

What Your Spouse Expects about Your Priorities

ALL THE EVEN-NUMBERED CHAPTERS of this book look at the expectations we bring to marriage and how they affect us. All of us get frustrated when our expectations are not met. So it's a good idea to understand where your spouse is coming from.

I'll direct part of every even-numbered chapter to women and part to men. So if you are a woman reading this book in the presence of your man, feel free to elbow him, bodycheck him, or put this book under his nose and say, "You need to read this." But let's keep it reasonable. Please don't put a sign in your yard that says, "Here lives an evil man." That's probably going just a little too far.

If you're a man, you may want to put a nice little lacy bookmark on the page of your choice and leave the book on your wife's bedside table. Maybe bring her a nice hot cup of decaf one night and suggest that she take a peek at the page you've marked.

I really do want you to talk about these ideas with each other because they won't do you much good if you read them in isolation. These expectations need to brought out into the open so your marriage can become all God intends it to be.

There are three major expectations a woman has in the area of priorities.

1. A Wife Expects Her Husband to Provide

When a woman hears a man say, "I do," on their wedding day, the number-one thing hidden deep in her heart is that she expects that man to provide for her.

A man's first responsibility to his wife is to provide. The husband is responsible to put the bread on the table. God said at the Fall that man would live by the sweat of his brow (see Gen. 3:19). If a woman wants to work, that's OK, assuming both parties have worked through the ramifications and can juggle those demands. The Bible doesn't say women shouldn't work. In Proverbs 31, an example is given of a woman who has income from two or three different sources—including real estate and clothing.

Our culture has shifted dramatically in this area. Since 1951, the labor force participation of wives has nearly tripled to 62 percent.[1] Be aware that the amount of hours a woman works correlates negatively to her overall marital satisfaction, especially if she would rather be at home.[2] This means that for many couples the cultural expectations of who provides for the family have changed. There is nothing wrong with a wife working, as long as both spouses understand that the man has the ultimate responsibility to provide.

The Hebrew in Genesis 3 can literally mean "men will have to work by the sweat of their nose." Have you been out in the yard in the summer, working hard for a couple of hours? You bend over with your hands on your knees to catch your breath and the sweat just drips off the end of your nose.

Part of the reason women live longer than men is that, historically, men have done the physical labor to provide. And then the Bible says that men are to give themselves for their wives like Christ gave himself for the church. So after we men work hard for about forty or fifty years, our wives bury us, get our insurance, marry a young guy, then kick back every summer in the mountains and every winter at the beach.

When I speak at retirement homes, there'll be sixty bright-eyed eighty-year-old ladies and two old guys scattered in the crowd. When I speak on marriage, I sometimes jokingly say that women do to men what Apaches used to do to horses. They ride 'em, lather 'em up, put 'em down, then go get another one. That's OK though because my wife already has my permission to find her a young gun when I'm gone.

In the Bible, Paul says, "If anyone does not provide for his own, . . . he has denied the faith and is worse than an unbeliever" (1 Tim. 5:8). It doesn't say, "If any woman," because that is not her responsibility. It is a man's responsibility to provide. What does it look like when a man doesn't provide?

Being Lazy

Have you ever seen a marriage that was in trouble because the man wouldn't work? It's a chronic problem—it just goes on and on and wears at you. Proverbs 26:14 says, "As the door turns on its hinges, / So does the sluggard on his bed." He'll turn over back and forth, but he won't get out of the bed and do anything. That kind of man is worthless—like an old mutt who lives under a porch. I can't tell you the number of times I have talked to women who were frustrated beyond belief because their husbands wouldn't get off the sofa.

Trying to Get Rich Quick

Other men are constantly looking for the next big thing. You'll always find a frustrated woman married to a guy who is always waiting for his ship to come in. He can't work Monday through Friday because he doesn't want to miss his "big score." These men are always into some neat, nifty scheme that's going to hit the jackpot. "Those who want to get rich fall into temptation and a snare" (1 Tim. 6:9). In Proverbs 28:22, the Bible talks about those who hasten after wealth, who want to get rich quick. A man's job is to steadily provide for his family.

Getting Strangled by Debt

When you have a man who isn't good with his debts, you'll have a woman who doesn't sleep at night. The Bible goes so far as to call this man evil: "The wicked borrows and does not pay back" (Ps. 37:21). Proverbs 22:7 says, "the borrower becomes the lender's slave." A woman expects a man to keep them from getting in debt over their heads.

Being All Talk and No Action

Proverbs also says, "In all labor there is profit, / But mere talk leads only to poverty" (14:23). Have you ever seen guys who like to talk about work a lot more than they like to work?

A woman expects her husband to be willing to do what needs to be done to have a decent career and provide for their family.

Wasting Money in Sin

The Bible says, "There is precious treasure and oil in the dwelling of the wise, / But a foolish man swallows it up" (Prov. 21:20). They take everything that comes in and blow it on stuff that doesn't matter. They don't manage their money and are always worried about how they are going to pay the rent.

Young women are often attracted to what we in counseling call "Peter Pans." They are happy-go-lucky and carefree young guys. They are funny, loose, and just sort of float through life. Women have a fascination with these type of men. These guys are rebellious; they don't like to be tied down. They're free spirits. And they're a lot of fun to be around for about six hours.

The problem is that they also don't work. They're not really responsible. They wake up at the crack of noon and fly by the seat of their pants in life. They are like Robin Williams in the movie *Mrs. Doubtfire.* Sally Field was attracted to Robin because he was cute, funny, and carefree. But what is fun for a few dates becomes miserable in a marriage. When you start having to put bread on the table and the kids through school, those type of guys just aren't that fun anymore. So I tell young women, "When you're selecting a mate, ask yourself, *Does this guy work? Can he get after it, be responsible, and do what he has to do?"*

2. A Wife Expects Her Husband to Help

Believe it or not, one of the things your wife was thinking when she said, "I do," was that she would have *help* around the house. When I teach on this, I always think about this wonderful couple in my church. He's a doctor. One day he thought he would be a little bit of a smart aleck after reading Proverbs 31:15 ("She rises also while it is still night / And gives food to her household / And portions to her maidens.") He asked his wife, "When are you going to start rising early to give food to your household?" She came right back: "When are you going to get me some of those maidens?"

A wife expects her husband to help around the house and to do chores. This is something that I have tried to take to heart. It took a lot of work, but I have become one of the great dishwasher-unloaders in the history of the world. Teresa likes it loaded a certain way, but I can unload that thing like it's an Olympic sport. I once heard Laura Schlessinger say, "To me the sound of vacuuming is foreplay." I want you to know I'm a vacuuming fool.

I do a pretty good job when my wife doesn't want to cook. I hustle out, get the stuff, and cook it up. To some women, having someone come in and clean for her once in a while would be heaven on earth. My wife is meticulous. If someone were coming to clean on a Monday, she would be cleaning all day Sunday to get ready. So I pitch in to help where I can.

Some men can help just by chilling out a little about the cleanliness of the house. If there's some interesting color on the food in the freezer, tell your wife to take a break and deal with it yourself. There's a relentlessness to caring for a house, and sometimes it helps just to let a woman get away. Tell your wife, "You go. I'll take care of things. Go out with your friends and do what you want to do. I'll take care of things right here."

In one sense, Paul gives a heavy load to all of us men: "Husbands, love your wives, just as Christ also loved the church" (Eph. 5:25). When men hear that, they immediately think, *The cross, crucifixion . . . I've got to be ready to die for my wife.* And so we prepare ourselves to be forced to die a slow and tortuous death for our wives.

If a truck were driving out of control straight at your wife, my guess is that every guy reading this book would grab her, pull her out of the way, and take the hit full on. If the bad guys came in your house, you're probably not going to push your wife out the bedroom door and tell her to yell if she finds anything. Men save their wives from mortal dangers.

But there are probably not going to be many times in your life when you're about to be run over by a truck. You almost certainly will not have to be martyred for your wife. And the problem is that for many men, martyrdom would be a lot easier than vacuuming. Martyrdom is easier than holding your wife's hand and saying, "Is there anything I can get for you?"

And so, to love your wife as Christ loved the church doesn't usually require some enormous act of martyrdom but rather a daily dying to yourself and giving yourself over to this woman. When your wife said, "I do," she was thinking that you would help out around the house.

3. A Wife Expects Her Husband to Lead

There's another thing a woman was looking for when she heard her husband say, "I do." A woman was expecting to marry a man who would be a leader. I never run into women who are looking for weak men. I've never heard a woman pray, "Oh, God, give me a wimp. Make him stupid, make him slow, make him a coward. Give me a failure."

I understand that women have reacted against a deviant version of a strong man. I call these "rogue males"—irresponsible or violent men—and we've all seen how women suffer at their hands.

But a woman still wants a strong man who's going someplace.

She doesn't want to be hitched to a man whom she always has to cajole and harangue. She doesn't want to be praying every day, "God, would you just light a fire under my husband? Whatever you've got to do, short of killing him, would you just do it to him, God?" A woman dreams about a man who is a courageous man, a responsible man, a godly man who leads her family, and who says, "Follow me."

Gloria Steinem said, "We women have finally become the men we always wanted to marry." There's a lot of truth to that. Women always wanted strong, assertive men but didn't get them, so they just became them. Husbands, God is calling you to be sacrificial leaders. Step up and do what needs to be done for the joy of your wife and the glory of Christ.

Men also have expectations when it comes to their wife's priorities in marriage. These expectations color how a man feels about his marriage and his connection to his wife.

1. A Husband Expects a Well-Managed House

Although it may sound a bit strange, when a man gets married, he expects to have a well-managed home. He expects to have an orderly and clean house. This may sound old-fashioned, but it's still true and it's still biblical. First Timothy says that women are to "keep house" (5:14). That's a bad translation. The word *house* actually meant everything associated with the household—including children, servants, property, and any business interests that took place in the home. Paul says a woman has control of her domicile. A man's responsibility is to provide. A woman's responsibility is her home.

When we moved into our new church, I let some of the women decorate and arrange my office. If it had been up to me, I would have just driven a nail and hung a dead animal on it. That's what men in Texas call decorating.

But I knew that my office was a place of ministry, and it needed to look appropriate. So I gave these women my stuff and said, "Take it and do what you want." It is amazing what they did with my study—it's a thing of beauty.

Obviously not all women are Martha Stewart, and not all men are Neanderthals. But a man does need to know that his house is in order. I've actually seen couples divorce because they couldn't agree on how to take care of their house.

In Titus 2:3–5, Paul says, "Older women likewise are to be reverent in their behavior, not malicious gossips nor enslaved to much wine, teaching what is good, so that they may encourage the young women to love their husbands, to love their children, to be sensible, pure, workers at home, kind, being subject to their own husbands, so that the word of God will not be dishonored."

It takes skill and training to care for a home. In ancient Israel, the book of Leviticus demonstrated the importance of keeping your bodies and homes clean. If you got a fungus on your wall, you cleaned it. Or you had it examined by the priest and had to take that part of the wall out. If the fungus continued to grow, you had to tear the house down. You had to keep your house clean.

If a spot started to grow on your clothes, you had to cut that part out and patch it. If the spot continued to grow, you had to destroy the garment.

Your food and utensils had to be clean. If you found a dead animal in any utensil, you destroyed the utensil. So Israel was the cleanest nation on the face of the earth.

During the Black Plague of the Middle Ages, the rumor began

that the Jews were poisoning the wells and causing the deaths. Why did people accuse the Jews? Some historians believe it's because there were fewer Jews dying during the plague. The plague was carried by fleas on rats. Since the Jewish homes were kosher, there was less filth for a rat to live on.

Today, I often counsel couples who are like Felix and Oscar from *The Odd Couple*. One of them could not care less how dirty the house is; the other needs it clean. You have to work together and compromise. And ultimately a woman needs to work it out so she can manage the house.

2. A Husband Expects the Family Will Remain His Wife's Top Priority

When a man marries, he expects the marriage and family will remain his wife's top priority. No man gets married hoping that his wife will one day care more about her career than the family. He's not wishing that she will be so wrapped up in volunteer activities that she can no longer manage their home. He's not thinking that her hobbies and interests will distract her to the point of no longer being able to function well as a wife and mother.

Men don't do well when they feel their children are being neglected by the one God designed to be the chief caregiver.

As we will see later, it's important for both a husband and a wife to be well-rounded people. But I've met some wives who allowed other things to take the central place in their lives that God intended for their families. This often happens with careers, but I've also seen it with athletic pursuits, hobbies, friendships, and volunteer activities.

I have even watched a woman bored with her husband and kids become obsessed with serving and working at the church. It got so bad that the neglected husband finally had to issue an ultimatum. This woman almost suffered a catastrophe.

Wives, is it clear to your husband and children that, after God, they are your most important priority? If not, you are on dangerous ground, and the foundation of your marriage is slowly being eaten away.

These expectations are important because they reveal our hearts and the priorities of our marriage.

How are you doing as a couple in the area of priorities? Use the discussion questions below to think through needed changes to have better love now.

Keeping the Fence Post Solid

Key Concepts about Your Priorities

- When a marriage goes south, it's because one or both spouses misplaced their priorities.
- Priorities determine whether your marriage is moving forward or backward.
- Key priorities include:
  - your individual time with God
  - your friendship
  - quality time together
  - good sex
  - direction for your marriage
  - your children
  - humility
  - repentance
- A wife expects her husband to provide.

- A wife expects her husband to help.
- A wife expects her husband to lead.
- A husband expects a well-managed house.
- A husband expects the family will remain his wife's top priority.

Straightening the Post

Discussion for Better Love Now

1. What are some ways couples get offtrack in terms of their priorities in our culture today? Which of these is the greatest temptation to you? Why?

2. Which of the priorities mentioned in chapter 1 is the most important to you in your marriage right now? Why? What changes need to be made in this area?

3. Do you agree with the expectations listed in chapter 2? Why or why not? How have you seen these in your marriage?

4. What is the most important thing God might want you to do differently in the next week to see a change in the area of priorities? How will you make that change?

Fence Post 2: Communication

Talk about a hot-button issue. I don't know a single couple who hasn't struggled at one time or another in the area of communication. How much do you talk? What do you talk about? Does your spouse feel valued and listened to? Does your spouse feel like you are never satisfied with what they say?

Communication is at the heart of marriage because it is one of the ways God allows us to grow into his image with one another. We experience and learn things by connecting with our spouse that we simply cannot receive any other way. That's part of why we have become one flesh—to share our lives and hearts with one another.

The next two chapters will help you improve the level of communication in your marriage. But first, have a short discussion to discover how you both think you're doing now in the area of communication.

Rate your marriage in the area of communication to jump-start your thinking about the topic. Have a short, ten-minute discussion with your spouse to prepare you for what God might want to do in your heart.

Fence Post 2: Communication

Wife's Perspective

How would you rate your marriage in the area of communication? Use the following to chart your thoughts.

With a pencil, draw a line on each fence post to show your rating for your marriage in the area of communication.

I am thrilled with how we communicate.

We just don't seem to connect.

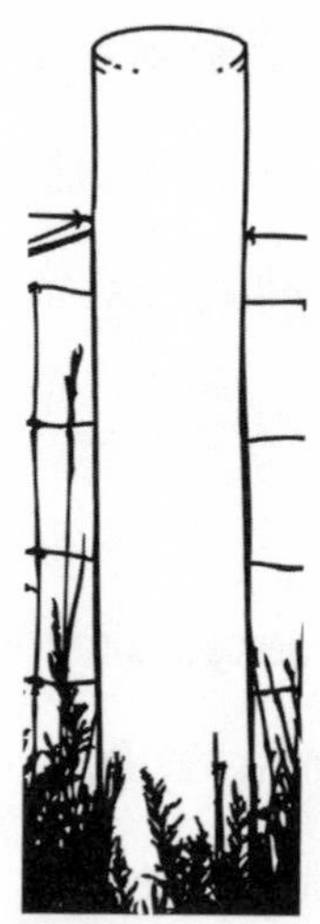

Step 1: As a wife, how would you rate your marriage in the area of communication?

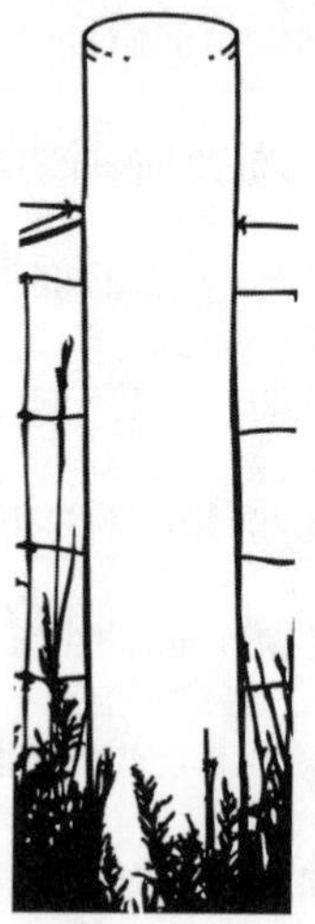

Step 2: How will your husband rate your marriage in the area of communication?

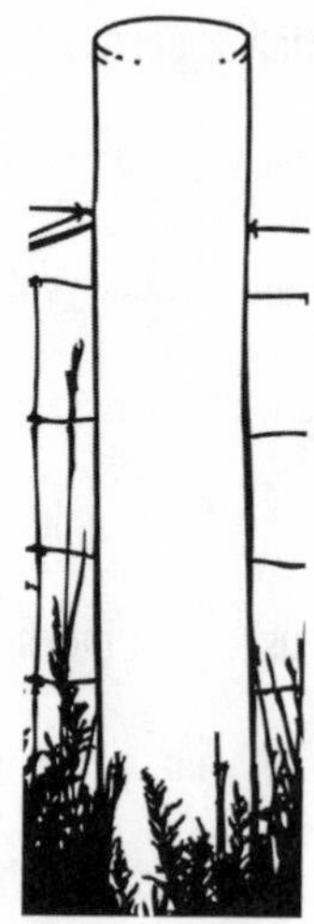

Step 3: What will your husband say you thought? Mark where he will say you rated your marriage's communication.

Fence Post 2: Communication

Husband's Perspective

As a husband, how would you rate your marriage in the area of communication? Use the following to chart your thoughts.

With a pencil, draw a line on each fence post to show your rating in the area of communication.

I am thrilled with how we communicate.

We just don't seem to connect.

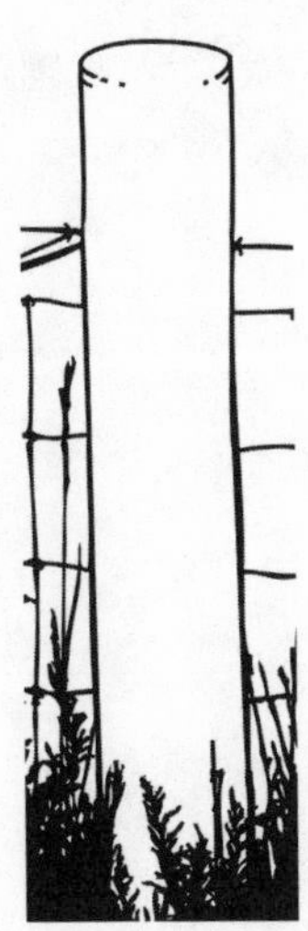

Step 1: As a husband, how would you rate your marriage in the area of communication?

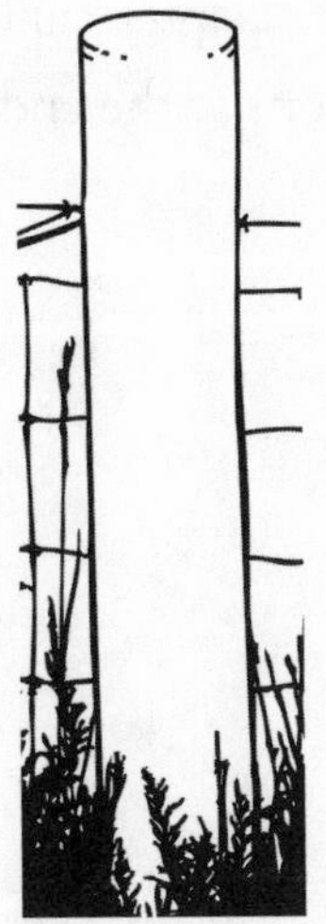

Step 2: How will your wife rate your marriage in the area of communication?

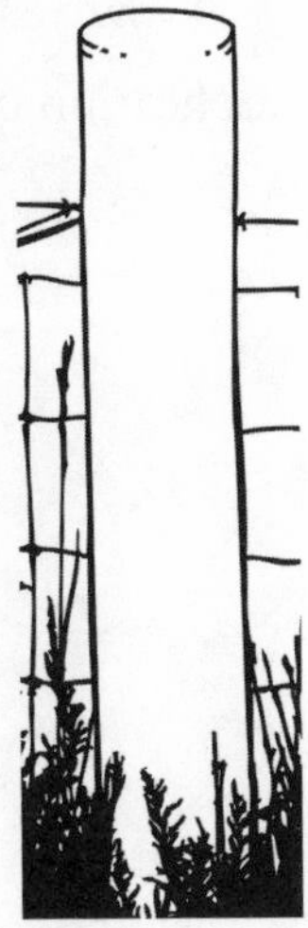

Step 3: What will your wife say you thought? Mark where she will say you rated your marriage's communication.

For Discussion:

Take about ten minutes and work your way from step 1 to step 3. For each step, share why you rated your communication the way you did. (Note that the wife's step 3 corresponds to the husband's step 2.)

What issues does this raise that you want to consider more deeply? Are there areas in which you and your spouse have a different perspective? Have you seen some potential areas of conflict that need to be addressed?

Have a short prayer, asking God to help you both change in any ways necessary to have better love now.

Now read the chapters and talk through the discussion and application questions at the end.

Chapter 3

Communicating to Have Better Love Now

SOMETIMES A COUPLE WILL sit in my office and say, "We just don't communicate anymore." No matter how many times they repeat it, I know it's not true. All couples communicate. The only question is whether they communicate well or poorly.

A person who turns and leaves the room in the middle of a discussion is communicating very clearly. Someone who ignores their spouse and keeps watching TV or surfing the Internet is talking loud and clear. Harsh words, raised voices, rolling your eyes, sarcastic comments, passive-aggressive tendencies—all these things communicate; they just communicate in a destructive way.

Why is communication such an important key to better love now? Communication is one of the foundations of any friendship. You talk to people whom you like, and you like people whom you talk to. In Song of Solomon 5:16, the woman says, "This is my beloved and this is my friend."

Think about one of your friends for a moment. How did you become friends? Think back to the first time you really interacted. You probably had a conversation where you talked and connected with each other. As you heard this person's heart, you were drawn to them, and you became friends.

The same thing was true when you met your spouse, and the same thing needs to be true in your marriage. Communication is fertilizer for friendship. If you don't communicate well, you'll forget why you thought this person was so fascinating and loveable.

Dr. John Gottman of the University of Washington has made a career out of watching the way couples communicate. He has videotaped the interactions of over 700 couples in his laboratory and studied their actions and reactions in meticulous detail.

After twenty-five years of research, he can now watch a five-minute video clip of a couple talking to one another and predict with 91 percent accuracy whether they will eventually divorce.[3]

How does he do it? He watches a couple's communication and looks for what he calls the *four horsemen*: criticism, contempt, defensiveness, and stonewalling. When a couple's communication degenerates in these ways, it reveals a fundamental shift of the heart.

Criticizing your mate demonstrates that you are no longer aligned with your spouse; you are now standing against them. When you speak to your mate with contempt, you make it clear that you believe the person you are talking to is of no worth. When you react with defensiveness, you show that your spouse is not worth being reconciled to. When you stonewall your mate, you make it clear that they are not worth listening to. Your communication shows that you no longer treasure your spouse.

If you read your Bible, it shouldn't surprise you that Dr. Gottman can learn so much from watching couples talk to one another. The Bible shows that our words are a direct display of what's going on in our heart. Jesus himself said, "The mouth speaks out of that which fills the heart" (Matt. 12:34). This is why Jesus can say, "By your words you will be justified, and by your words you will be condemned" (Matt. 12:37). What you say and how you communicate is a direct reflection of what is going on in your heart. Your spouse instinctively knows this. That's why communication is so critical.

Of course, no marriage is a ceaseless stream of blissful communication. Every couple is going to disagree, argue, hurt feelings, and have conflict. So how do you maintain good communication even when you and your spouse aren't seeing eye to eye? If you can communicate successfully through conflict, your marriage will be stronger in both the stormy and the sunny days.

Years ago I heard a man talking about his marriage. After he and his wife had an argument, he said, "My wife whipped off her wedding ring and threw it. It disappeared into the floor. She was horrified. So she and I got down on our knees with a fork, and we dug it out of a crack in the boards, laughing about our sin." The man who told that story? Francis Schaeffer, perhaps the leading Christian thinker of the last half of the twentieth century.

Another man spoke one time about how his wife was so angry that she went to the garage and got in their car to drive away from the house. He stood between the car and the street, knowing that she probably wouldn't kill him. She said she looked at him in the rearview mirror as she began to back out and thought, *I wonder if this would be first-degree or manslaughter?* She decided she'd better stop. That story was told by Dr. and Mrs. Bill Bright, the founders of Campus Crusade for Christ.

I also heard a man talk about the time he was speaking at a marriage conference. He surprised his wife with the fact that she was scheduled to do a small-group seminar. She wasn't prepared, so she said, "If you ever do this again, I'm going to stand you up and not show."

"Oh, yeah?"

"Yeah!"

"Well, oh yeah?"

"Yeah!"

And they drove home from the marriage conference in dead silence from San Antonio to Dallas. That story was told by Mr. and Mrs. Howard Hendricks.

All marriages have conflict. Unless your spouse was virgin-born and is the incarnation of a deity, you'll have conflict. If you married a human, a child of Adam, you married a fallen person. Your marriage will have conflict; the issue is what you will do with the conflict when it occurs.

Some couples handle conflict with dignity and respect. They learn from it, apologize, change, and grow. That's called fighting clean. Good marriages are not good because the couples never have fights. They are good because both people have a fundamental belief that the other person and the marriage are more important than their own desires.

Some marriages don't handle conflict as well. They fight dirty. They cast away the peace of their home. Each person feels like they have to win. And they will destroy their marriage in trying to change the other person to conform to their twisted vision. But they will not change themselves.

In some marriages, each spouse ultimately draws the other closer by imitating the humility and winsomeness of Christ. In other marriages, spouses repel the other by alienating them and demanding their own way in every situation.

So what are the rules of engagement in marriage? How do you deal with conflict? If you can't communicate through conflict, the fence post of your marriage will rot from the inside out. I've discussed this topic in detail in *The Book of Romance*, but it's so important that I want to give an overview again here. Here are seven principles for fighting well and having better love now.

1. Don't React

When—not if—your mate offends you, remember they probably didn't just sit down and say, "You know, I think I'll play the devil today." No, they did something in their ignorance and their sinfulness that they felt was OK, but it wasn't. They were just acting like a normal human being. So whenever your mate hurts you, don't react. And I use that term very precisely. Don't re-act. Don't take their action and mirror it. If you do, they will want to respond in kind, and you'll end up playing emotional tennis. That's a game nobody wins. It's like when you're mowing your lawn, and you catch some baling wire in the blade. Pretty soon the blade is wrapped up so tight that it won't work.

The same thing happens when conflict escalates in marriage. I've seen couples who don't even like each other anymore. They won't even speak except to go back and forth, making a point about why they are right.

I've never seen a situation where a spouse does something wrong, then their husband or wife yells and slams the door, and then the offending spouse says, "Woo, that hurt. I repent. Jesus, lead me." That never happens. The offending spouse is thinking, *I'm glad I hurt you; you deserved being hurt if you're going to act like that.* So don't react and mimic the action of your mate.

I know this is hard for us to grasp, but when your mate offends you, the entire fabric of the universe won't be ripped apart if you don't bring immediate judgment on their head. It really won't. "While being reviled, He did not revile in return; while suffering, He uttered no threats, but kept entrusting Himself to Him who judges righteously" (1 Pet. 2:23). That's Peter writing about Jesus, and Peter was there to witness it all.

What about this version? "And they spat upon Jesus. Jesus, spitting back in their faces, said, 'I know you, fool, and I'm returning and you're going to end up in hell.'" Would that look just a little bit odd? Christ didn't react and allow himself to be pulled down to the level of everybody else.

2. Don't Chasten and Try to Change

This is sometimes hard for us to remember: even if we are great spouses, we are lousy deities. Don't take the place of God and the Holy Spirit. You can't change your mate by punishing them. I've seen people who don't react right away in conflict, but they think, *Maybe I didn't get you during this conflict, but I'll get you by special ops. I'll go after you when you least expect it.* And they give their mate the silent treatment or humiliate them in public or cut them off sexually.

Don't chasten your mate. Instead, let them see Christ. Paul said if your enemy's hungry, feed him. If he's thirsty, give him a drink, and in so doing you heap burning coals upon their head. Whenever you do evil to others and they are kind in response, their godliness becomes a crystal-clear mirror that shows you your evil.

I have found that when couples are in the throes of a divorce, the more guilty of the pair will incite the less guilty to anger and wrath. That anger salves their guilty conscience. The more kind the other party is, the worse the offender feels.

Willie Nelson went through a number of marriages. He tells a story about one of his early marriages when he had a drinking problem. After his wife had lectured him over and over, he still came home drunk and flopped on a cot. She'd had it with him. She took the sheet he was on and turned it back over him, then sewed up the perimeter, turning him into a little Willie-burrito. Then she took a mop, unscrewed the handle, and began to beat him. She'd get tired, set it down, and watch a little TV, then come back and beat him some more. And Willie just kept on drinking.

Another story is told about the time the wind and the sun got in a quarrel about who was the strongest. They saw a traveler coming down the road and agreed that whoever could get the hat and scarf off this traveler would be considered the mightiest. The wind took his turn first. He blew seventy miles an hour, but the traveler just pulled his hat tighter and put another knot in his scarf.

Then it was the sun's turn. The sun slowly got brighter and brighter. Eventually, the man warmed up enough that he willingly took off his hat and scarf. I didn't invent this story. It's from Aesop, who in about 300 BC recognized, even apart from Scripture, that you can't change people by dominating them. If they change, it's in the presence of warmth and grace.

3. Resolve to Resolve

In conflict, your attitude can't be "I'm going to win." It's not you against your spouse. It's both of you against the conflict. Your attitude should be "I'm going to take this thing that has come up between us, and together we're going to isolate it, kill it, and bring peace."

When you're offended by a stranger and you respond in anger, you can walk away without too many consequences (other than losing your reputation and testimony). But that doesn't work in marriage because you've got to share a bedroom and a den and a living room and a bathroom and a kitchen—you can't afford to alienate that person. You have to resolve that "we are going to fix this no matter what."

The turning point of conflict in your marriage is when you say, "I choose to change me in order to fix this thing. I will not say that only my mate has to change. I am not going to preserve my pride and cause all kinds of problems in my home because I am not willing to change." As simple as that sounds, when I counsel couples, it's pretty easy to put them into two groups. Some are willing to say, "I'll change because I want to fight for my marriage." Others say, "To heck with the home. There's only one important person here, and you're looking at him. *You* need help because you're causing these problems."

4. Talk

I consistently run into men who believe that submission means silence. That's not true at all. Submission doesn't mean that your wife lets you get away with evil. And being a loving leader as a man doesn't mean that you avoid sitting your wife down to say, "Baby, we've got a problem."

Even after you don't react, after you don't try to manipulate your mate, after you resolve to bring a resolution, you still have to talk to one another. If you're the offended party, there's a correct way to bring things up with your mate. You could say to him, "Yo, idiot, come here." You could say to her, "Queen of the Harpies, could

I speak to you for just a minute here?" But if you start a conversation like that, you immediately put your mate on the defensive. Proverbs 25:15 says, "By forbearance a ruler may be persuaded, / And a soft tongue breaks the bone."

If someone came into my office and said, "I've been here a few months, and I've really got a bone to pick with you," I can guarantee you I would win that argument. I'd try to be nice, but even if I'm wrong, he won't win because I am not going to let a person I don't know come in and challenge the position of the pastor.

But if a person comes to me and says, "You know, y'all are doing such a good job. This church is such a blessing. God is really using you in my life. I had a thought I wanted to share with you. I see an area where we could possibly improve, and I'm willing to do whatever I need to do to be a part of the solution," I will have a totally different reaction. He's on my side, and he wants what's best for the church.

"A gentle answer turns away wrath, / But a harsh word stirs up anger" (Prov. 15:1). Speak gently when you begin to deal with conflict. And when your spouse voices a concern, let the adrenaline settle before you respond. Let the hormones go back to their place. Just wait a few seconds. Think and pray. Don't escalate the conflict with attacks or excuses. Don't interrupt and say, "Get to the end of it. Hurry up." Don't turn it around on your spouse: "Well, you're not perfect. Remember yesterday?"

If you throw the grievance back in your spouse's face, you've put them in a very difficult position. What will they be thinking? *I'm not getting an audience. Maybe I need to turn up the volume. Do I throw something? Do I yell? Do I have to make this a pitched battle?*

I've met a lot of people who are experts at turning conflict around until their mate says, "No, I just quit. You won't listen.

It's not worth it; you can win." But that's not a peaceful home. The law of survival took over. The big guy ate the little guy, and the little guy gave up and let him win. The weaker is ruled by the stronger, and now evil has settled into that home. You have a new tenant in your house—Satan.

What about a man who is consistently put down by an overbearing woman? He'll stay quiet, but he doesn't respect her anymore. There won't be any kindness or passion. Seldom will anyone desire to make love to a person who runs them over and treats them badly. He starts thinking, *I've made a long-term mistake.*

When you don't resolve conflicts gently, communication ends, and you become two empty shells in the relationship. The wife becomes a maid and a cook; the husband becomes a butler and a mechanic. That's not marriage. No one dreamed of a life like that when they were standing at the altar on their wedding day.

When your mate hurts, they need hope. And hope comes when you really listen to them. My wife knows I am not perfect, and that's OK. But I have to be "perfect-able." She knows I'm not Christ, but I've got to be becoming more Christlike. I've got to be willing to flex and say, "If there's a problem, I'm going to bend. I'm not going to force you to be shaped into my own image." So I've got to listen and I've got to change.

In the Bible, King David is called a man after God's own heart. David was a man who knew how to handle a rebuke. Nathan rebuked him and he changed. Joab, his enemy, rebuked him, and David changed. A wise woman from Tekoa rebuked him about Absalom, and he changed. Shimei, who was going to be executed, rebuked him, and David said, "Maybe I need rebuking, let him alone." Abigail rebuked him, and David relented. That's why he's called the man after God's own heart. He wanted God to be pleased. That's why he could say, "Let the righteous smite me in kindness and reprove me; it is oil upon the head; do not let my head refuse it" (Ps. 141:5).

A good actor doesn't just recite the script when his fellow actor is finished speaking. The production would be staccato and boring. A good actor learns his lines and listens when the other actor is speaking. He listens so that his lines meld with what that person feeds him. The dialogue sounds natural because he really listens.

That's the way you become a good mate. You melt into the heart of your spouse when they speak to you. When your mate says, "I'm hurting," you remove your six-guns from their holsters and calmly lay them down. You don't roll your eyes, give a big sigh, or cross your arms. You look your spouse in the eye and say, "Talk to me. What did I do?"

5. Apologize

What separates a fool and a wise man? The Bible says one of the clearest indicators is their response to sin.

The wisdom of the sensible is to understand his way,
    But the foolishness of fools is deceit.
Fools mock at sin,
    but among the upright there is good will. (Prov. 14:8–9)

A fool ignores his sin or acts like it is no big deal. A wise man realizes sin has to be dealt with quickly and thoroughly. So when my wife says, "That hurt," I've got to turn to her and earnestly say, "Baby, I'm sorry. I didn't mean it to come out that way, but it did. I was just insensitive. Would you forgive me?"

This one is from personal experience. I can't tell you how many times the following scenario has happened in my marriage:

"Tommy, do you know what you just did?"

"What, baby?"

"You did this."

"Did I really? I'm sorry. Would you forgive me?"

"Yes."

6. Forgive

Forgiveness is such an important aspect of having better love now that we will look at it in detail in a later chapter, but I need to mention it now in relationship to conflict. When your spouse apologizes, resist the temptation to play God and bring justice into the situation. Remember the story of Joseph? Joseph's brothers came to him after his father, Jacob, had died. These are the same brothers who sold him into slavery. Now that their daddy was dead, they told Joseph, "We're afraid that you're going to kill us now." What was Joseph's reply? "Am I God?" Translation: "It's not my job."

Paul tells us that God says, "VENGEANCE IS MINE, I WILL REPAY" (Rom. 12:19). Let God worry about making everything right. You focus on forgiveness and restoration of the relationship.

7. Grow

It's a strange time when a couple stands in front of me to get married. When a man and woman are getting married, they are like deer in the headlights. I can make them say anything. If I said, "I will give you, Pastor Nelson, all my money, all my retirement," back it would come: "I will give you, Pastor Nelson, all my money, all my retirement."

When I say, "I'll love, honor, and cherish you as Christ does the church," they come right back: "I will love, honor, and cherish you as Christ does the church." Do they really know what they're talking about? No. But they are about to learn.

When your mate says, "That hurt me," and you say, "I'm sorry," and they say, "I forgive you," what happens next? This last step in conflict is the most important. Without this, you'll be trapped in the same old cycles throughout your marriage.

You have to amend your life for the delight of your mate and the pleasure of God. That is called change. You have to grow. You're about to have a chance to do all the things you vowed you were going to do but didn't know you were agreeing to when you made that vow.

In those moments you'll learn why Martin Luther said, "Marriage did for me what no monastery could." You can study the Bible all you want as a single person, but you won't discover all your junk until you get married. Getting married is like climbing into a vat of 212-degree water. You get boiled and your stuff rises to the surface. Only now will you see all the trashy stuff in yourself, and your mate will reflect it in their tears and pain.

So when your spouse points out a problem, compare it against the standard, yield, apologize, forgive, and then change. When you do that, you are imitating Christ. And that looks good on a human. Apologizing, repentant people are beautiful. They are noble. It makes you love them more.

So be willing to make an alteration. If a guy is supposed to be home for dinner at six but doesn't come home until seven and didn't call his wife, she will say, "It sat there waiting. Baby, you have to call me." He will make a note to either be there at six next time or make darn sure he calls to let her know he'll be late. It's not enough to keep repenting; you need to change whatever it was that hurt her.

If the husband says to the wife, "You just said something that humiliated me in public, honey, and you didn't realize how that made me feel," the wife can't make excuses by saying, "You're too sensitive." She just learned something about God, righteousness, marriage, her mate, and herself. She's about to grow, but she's got to be open to making a change.

When the husband says, "I looked at my checkbook and it's missing $600. I don't mind you spending it, just let me know when there's going to be a big expenditure." Make a note. Communicate. Change. That's what makes for a great marriage. Conflicts let you learn about your mate, God, marriage, and you.

Whenever you humble yourself to change and do what's best for your spouse rather than what you desire, that's called love. That's what love is.

I chuckle sometimes at these Hollywood guys who've been through about four wives and then talk about being great lovers. As soon as a woman no longer caters to them, they punt her for another one. It doesn't matter about her, marriage, or the kids—they're the only one who is important. A guy like that doesn't have a clue about love.

You show me some guy and some woman who have learned to live in peace, to deal with sin, and to improve their lives for about sixty years, and I'll read their book every time. They understand love. Follow their lead in conflict and you'll keep the heart of your marriage strong. Dealing with conflict well can help you have better love now.

Chapter 4

What Your Spouse Expects Concerning Communication

SOLOMON KNEW THAT "SWEETNESS of speech increases persuasiveness" (Prov. 16:21). It matters how you talk to your spouse. There is an art to speaking to your mate. You have to maintain a kind of formality and dignity of language in marriage. There ought to be things you will never say to your spouse and a tone of voice in which you would never speak.

We all know these unspoken guidelines instinctively when we first start out with our spouses. During those crucial first few weeks and months together, there is a filter on our mouths. Before we speak, we ask ourselves, "How is my beloved going to feel when they hear this?" We think before we speak, and we speak in a way that honors and uplifts our spouse.

Too many couples lose this consideration for one another as time goes by. They think that once they are married, they don't have to try so hard anymore. They refuse to couch their words or be careful how they speak.

I counsel people regularly who justify this lack of consideration and make it sound holy. They are proud of their ability to say what they feel. "I'm just the kind of person who speaks my mind; I don't play games," they say—as if a self-centered, uncontrolled tongue is a virtuous gift.

The Bible never tells us to say what we think or feel. The Bible says to stop talking before you say what you feel. God tells us to ponder before we respond to another person because our words matter. "There is one who speaks rashly like the thrusts of a sword, / But the tongue of the wise brings healing" (Prov. 12:18).

"Like apples of gold in settings of silver / Is a word spoken in right circumstances" (Prov. 25:11). In marriage, it's true you should be able to say almost anything to your spouse—if you do it in the right way, at the right time, and with the right tone. You can say some really tough things to someone when they know that you love them.

Marriage is friendship at its highest, so communicate with your spouse like you would with your best friend. Be gentle in how you speak. Remember that communication is more about really listening than it is talking. Use every interaction as an opportunity to communicate worth and value to your spouse.

This area of communication can be a minefield in marriage. I hear it all the time from couples in my church. "My husband won't talk to me." "My husband tries to fix things and give me quick answers." "All my wife ever wants to do is talk." And one of my personal favorites: "My wife would argue with a post."

Much of the confusion and difficulty in communication comes from the differing expectations of husbands and wives. When a woman is standing at the altar and hears her husband say, "I do," she has certain expectations about how he will communicate. When a man is standing at the altar and hears his wife say, "I do," he often has very different expectations about how they will communicate. Let's work on having better love now by getting these expectations out in the open and understanding where they come from.

Communication is one of the most important aspects of marriage for a woman. If you want to have better love now, do a better job communicating with your wife.

What is your wife looking for in the area of communication?

A Wife Expects a Listening Ear

When your wife heard you say, "I do," she expected that you were going to listen to her. She thought she was marrying a man who had a listening ear.

True confession time: I'm *terrible* on this. I remember one time early in my marriage when my wife was hurting about something. She began to share her heart while I was watching something on TV. So I glanced at her and then back to the TV. Each time I glanced at her, I would say, "um" or "huh" or "oh" or "yeah." All of a sudden I felt this cold, iron grip on my face. She grabbed me and turned my head toward her and said, "Listen to me with your face." I never forgot that, and I definitely needed to hear it.

Like most men, I have a quarterback mentality. What do I mean by that? I really was a quarterback in college. I proudly led our team to seven wins in my four years at North Texas. Even though we lost a lot of games, I still loved being a quarterback.

The players got in the huddle, then I walked in and nobody talked but me. Before I talked, however, everyone else bowed their head and listened carefully, thank you. I *loved* it. I would call the play, but nobody left yet because I wasn't ready. *Then* I would say, "Ready, break." They would all run to the line, while I walked, thank you. The players all bowed again at the line of scrimmage. Before we ran the play, I'd dry my hands on the center's butt. "Hut." Nobody moved, not yet. If they moved, it was a penalty because I wasn't ready yet. "Hut." I was just kidding. "Hut." I would drop back to pass, and they'd have to protect me and not let me get hit. I'd throw the ball, and then they couldn't hit me because it'd be a penalty. I'd make a complete pass; everyone would cheer for me. That's the life of a quarterback.

The problem is most men go into marriage thinking they are the quarterback and all the other members of the family are the offensive linemen. Teresa disabused me of that notion. Men, you need to snap back to reality and listen to your wives. The universe does not revolve around you.

Song of Solomon 8:13 says, "Companions are listening for your voice—Let me hear it!" That's one of the most amorous verses in the whole book of the Song of Solomon. "Companions are listening; let me hear it. Talk to me. I'm your best friend." Those are beautiful words to a woman.

If you ever lived life as a pagan, you probably remember some of the ways you tried to hustle a woman. (If you're a single guy reading this, please don't take notes on this section.) You go to a bar, you find a hurting girl, and what do you do? You listen. When she starts talking softly, you lean forward and look into her eyes. "That's terrible . . . then what happened?"

Nothing is more amorous to a woman than a man who really listens. Sometimes as a man, you need to shut down everything you are doing and focus on your wife. I have to do this as a discipline. I try to turn off the TV or put down the book and look straight at my wife, "Talk to me." What does she want? She wants me to listen. Do I know the answers? Yes (at least, I think I do). Does she want the answers? No. She just wants me to listen. Do I know why she's hurting? No. Does she know why she's hurting? No. Does God know? Yes. But she just wants to talk, and she wants me to listen. When your wife said, "I do," she expected to get a listening ear.

A Wife Expects to Get Her Husband's Heart

When she gets married, a wife also expects to get her husband's heart. When she says, "How was your day?" a woman really wants to know the answer. "How was your day?" means "I want to get inside of you. What were you doing when you were outside of our home? How will it affect our life and our family? What were you thinking about? What matters to you? I don't want to just monitor the events of our lives; I want to know what's going on in your mind and heart."

It's easy for men to be flippant about that question: "Aw, you know, I just saw some people, and there are some humans, people I work with, and we did stuff, and, um, you know. It was all right." (All spoken while staring at the computer screen.) A woman has to have her husband's heart.

I counseled a young lady recently who said, "He comes home and sits in the back room in the dark in front of the television." It frustrates her to no end. She wants her husband's heart; she wants to get inside of him, to learn what's he thinking.

When a woman connects with a man and hears about his thoughts, motivations, and desires, intimacy is created. Women often feel close to the people who listen to them and communicate with them at a level beyond surface interaction.

Men, we need to let our wives inside our hearts. Here's a practical idea: make a point every day to note one thing—an event that happened, an article that spawned a thought, a question you had to answer, a need that made you think—and then be sure to share it with your wife that evening.

It's not always easy to give your wife your heart, but it's a huge part of loving her as Christ loved the church.

A man also has expectations regarding communication, and it's important that husbands and wives get on the same page.

A Husband Expects to Communicate at the Right Time

James Dobson says that most people share about 25,000 words a day. A man goes to work and blows off about 20,000 of them. He gets home and his wife has saved up about 20,000 of them. She's spent 300 words on the kids, and now, she wants a mature, college graduate to talk with. She's ready to visit. And so the man, who's already shot his stuff, has to sit down and listen to his wife.

So here's a little advice for wives. When your husband comes home from work, don't meet him at the door with a child under your arm, "Beat this child. Beat him long and beat him hard. Beat him unto the fear of God." No, just meet him at the door and bring him in and feed him. Let him "veg" for just a little bit and make that transition. Give him some space and a few minutes to decompress.

Then you can carry the child under your arm and tell him to be the agent of God's justice. Then you can ask him about his day. After dessert, you can talk about that important decision that needs to be made about the house.

A man expects to be able to communicate at the appropriate time.

Also, be careful not to bring up embarrassing or delicate subjects in public. Sitting with another couple at a restaurant is not the time to chide your husband for eating another piece of bread or ordering dessert. He's put in a difficult situation: his natural instinct is to defend himself, but he won't want to do that in front of other people.

If you have an issue with your husband, speak to him privately. Give him a fair chance to consider your words and respond in a way that is appropriate.

A Husband Expects to Get the Benefit of the Doubt

Often wives think the worst of their husbands in the area of communication. Because many men don't talk as much as their wives would like, women can sometimes not appreciate what their husbands are actually saying.

Expectations can be dangerous. If a woman focuses on all she is not receiving in the area of communication, she can have a hard time appreciating the interactions she does have with her husband.

When a man shares something or has a serious discussion with his wife, it's discouraging to him if he doesn't receive encouragement. There is nothing more deflating to a man than to work hard at communicating, only to have his wife say, "It's about time we had a serious discussion. Guess I'll mark the calendar for another three years."

A wife needs to accept communication in the way her husband gives it and not always ask him to live up to her expectations.

A husband expects to get credit for trying to talk with his wife about what is important to him. He expects to get the benefit of the doubt. He wants to feel like his wife is on his side, wanting him to succeed, not expecting him to fail.

How are you all doing in the area of communication? It's a small thing, but it can make all the difference between a love that grows stronger each day and one that grows cold. Communicate with your spouse out of love for them and out of your love for God.

Use the following exercises and discussion questions to help you have better love now.

Keeping the Fence Post Solid

Key Concepts about Communication

- All couples communicate. The only question is whether they communicate well or badly.
- Communication is fertilizer for friendship.
- Avoid criticism, contempt, defensiveness, and stonewalling.
- If you can't communicate through conflict, the fence post of your marriage will rot from the inside out.
- A wife expects a listening ear.
- A wife expects to get her husband's heart.
- A husband expects to communicate at the right time.
- A husband expects to get the benefit of the doubt in communication.

Straightening the Post

Discussion for Better Love Now

1. What are you and your mate doing well in the area of communication? In what area of communication could you use more work?

2. How well do you and your mate deal with conflict? Which of the principles given in chapter 3 would be most important for you to work on?

3. Do you agree with the expectations listed in chapter 4? Why or why not? How have you seen these in your marriage?

4. What is the most important thing God might want you to do differently in the next week to see a change in the area of communication? What is one concrete step you could take to make that change?

Fence Post 3: Your Life Together

Roll over and take a look at the person next to you in the bed. Do you know how many more times you are going to wake up next to him or her? If you are married forty more years, that would be almost 15,000 times. Wow. You better make sure you know how to get along with each other.

Marriage is all day every day, and a huge part of making it work is learning how to live with one another. So many people struggle because they don't give and take in the daily issues of life. They never learn how to truly build a life together.

The next two chapters will help you evaluate how you are doing on a daily basis with your spouse in the mundane but important areas of life. But first, have a short discussion to gauge how you both think you're doing now in your life together.

I'm going to ask you to rate your marriage in the area of your life together. As with the previous sections, my goal is to get you thinking about each area before you read what I've written and what the Bible says. Have a short, ten-minute discussion with your spouse to prepare you for what God might want to do in your heart.

Fence Post 3: Your Life Together

Wife's Perspective

How would you rate your marriage in the area of your life together? Use the following to chart your thoughts.

With a pencil, draw a line on each fence post to show your rating for your marriage in the area of your life together.

Our life together is blissful and smooth.

Every day is a real struggle.

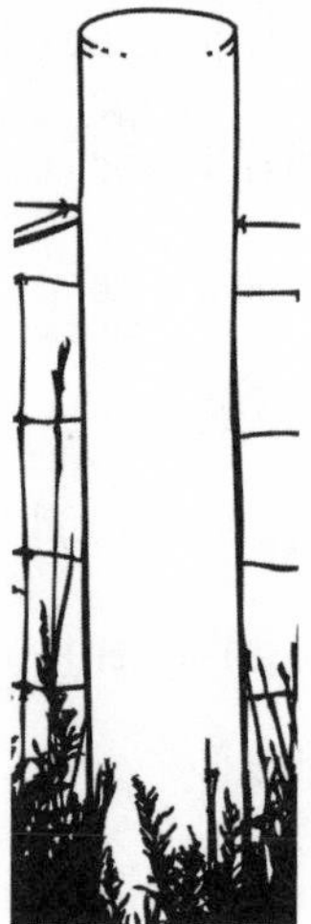

Step 1: As a wife, how would you rate your marriage in the area of your life together?

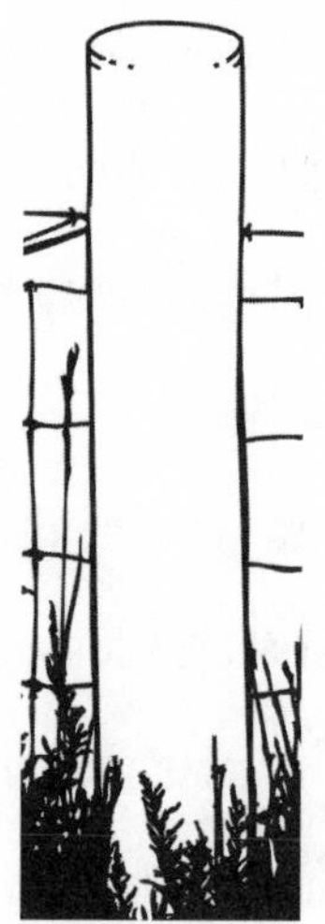

Step 2: How will your husband rate your marriage in the area of your life together?

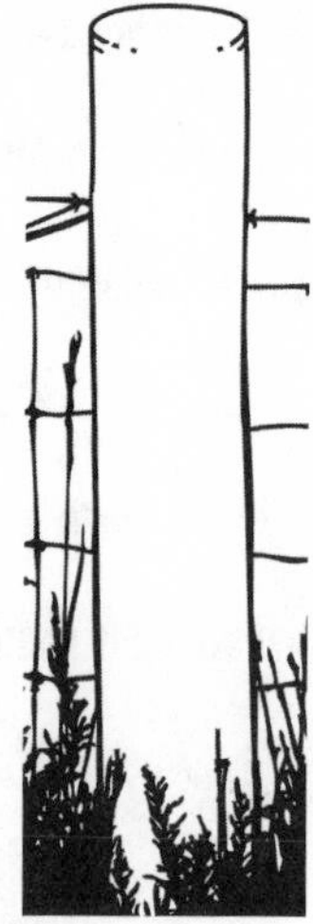

Step 3: What will your husband say you thought? Mark where he will say you rated your marriage in the area of your life together.

Fence Post 3: Your Life Together

Husband's Perspective

As a husband, how would you rate your marriage in the area of your life together? Use the following to chart your thoughts.

With a pencil, draw a line on each fence post to show your rating in the area of your life together.

Our life together is blissful and smooth.

Every day is a real struggle.

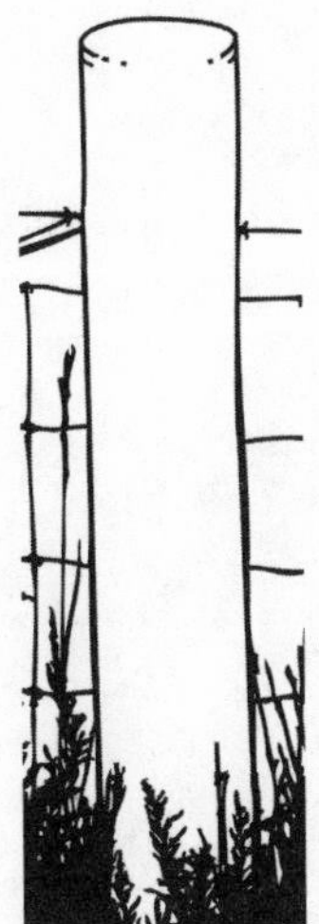

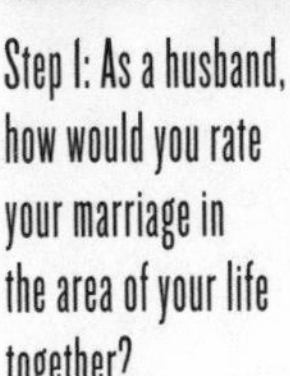

Step 1: As a husband, how would you rate your marriage in the area of your life together?

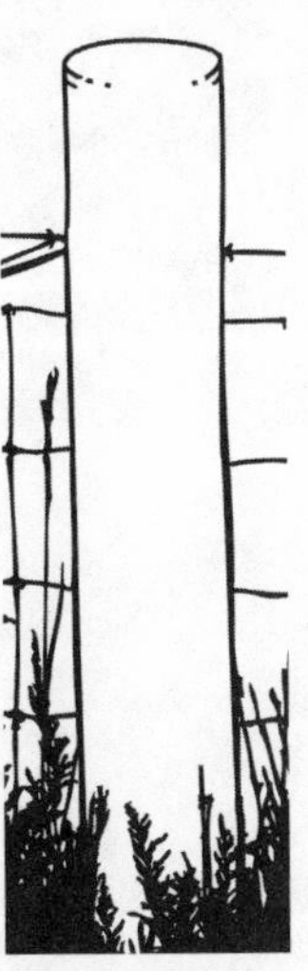

Step 2: How will your wife rate your marriage in the area of your life together?

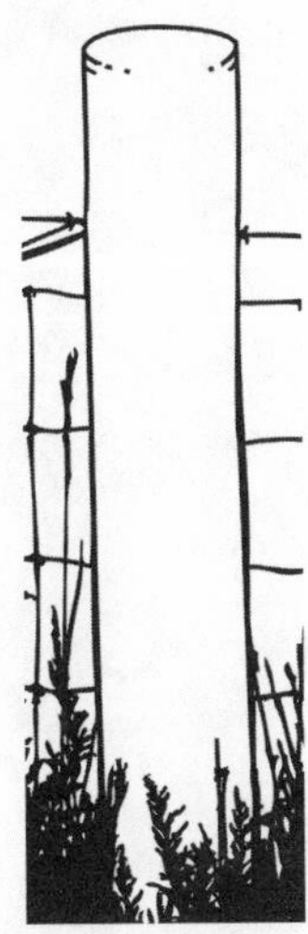

Step 3: What will your wife say you thought? Mark where she will say you rated your marriage in the area of your life together.

For Discussion:

Take about ten minutes and work your way from step 1 to step 3. For each step, share why you rated your life together the way you did. (Note that the wife's step 3 corresponds to the husband's step 2.)

What issues does this raise that you want to consider more deeply? Are there areas in which you and your spouse have a different perspective? Have you seen some potential areas of conflict that need to be addressed?

Have a short prayer, asking God to help you both change in any ways necessary to have better love now.

Now read the chapters and talk through the discussion and application questions at the end.

Chapter 5

Living Together

We have a number of folks in our church who homeschool their children. I think it's wonderful when parents take an active role in their kids' education, whatever the format. One of the benefits to homeschooling children is flexibility in planning their schedules. They can organize field trips, go out to breakfast with Dad, and help Mom with ministry at the church.

Many of these children eventually enter public or private schools. When they do, most of these children experience some culture shock. It's not what you think—they know how to behave and get along with other kids and all those things. The culture shock usually relates to the structure and relentlessness of an institutional school setting. You go to class all day every day. Each day is the same. Homework is due every day. Some classes have quizzes every day. There is often a period of adjustment as a homeschooled student gets used to this new environment.

Marriage can be like that. When you are dating, you see the best of each other. You only get together after you've prepared—guys have showered and put on deodorant; girls have done their hair and put on makeup. You'll spend two or three hours together and then go your separate ways.

When you marry, all of a sudden you are living with this other person twelve to fourteen hours a day. You are sharing a kitchen, bedroom, and bathroom. You discover each other's annoying habits, smell bad breath, and see hair lying in the bottom of the shower (gotta love that).

Marriage is relentless in its togetherness. It's day after day after day after day. Biblically, the only end in sight is when one of you puts the other in a pine box. You are stuck with each other. So it's important that you learn how to do life together in ways that help you have better love now.

In a sense this whole book helps you have a better daily life together, but one area is so important that we're going to take some time to focus on it in this chapter.

Money and Marriage

Money is like a land mine in marriage—it lies quietly in the field, until one day you step on it a certain way and it explodes. Problems with money fester over time, bringing feelings of distrust and disrespect. These feelings can easily turn into alienation in marriage.

I'd like to give you thirteen quick biblical principles on money in marriage.[4] Not only are these found in the Bible; they're also found in real life. When I thought about each of these, I remembered a particular face and a historical conflict that I'd had to deal with in counseling. If you get these straight, it will save you all kinds of heartache in your marriage.

1. It's Our Money

"I'm the one working hard to earn the money around here, so I get to decide how we spend it." "You'd think I could get a little respect, considering that I'm the one who makes the money to keep this family going." Whenever I hear statements like these from a couple, it is a telltale sign that marriage problems are on the way. It doesn't matter if the husband works and the wife doesn't, or if they both work—it's still all "our money." Neither spouse should say, "It's my money."

In my own situation, my wife does not have a job outside the home that produces income. But that makes no difference. "The two become one flesh." If a woman has a career that outearns her husband, it doesn't matter. It's not your money, it's "y'all's" money.

So even though my wife doesn't make money, she can spend money however she sees fit on the maintenance and the care of our home because it's our money. The two are one.

2. Agree on Major Expenditures

I'll never forget what a woman said to me: "He will not give me the freedom to buy a $14 dress pattern, but he will come home with $800 in tires. Somehow that's OK for him, but it's not OK for me." Even though it's *our* money, check with your mate before you make a major expenditure.

You don't want to surprise your mate in the area of money. Always check with your spouse, especially when you're about to charge a major expenditure. Trust me, if the credit company or the bank surprises your mate with what you did, that's not a good thing. Independence in the area of money is really a lack of respect, and it causes hurt and pain. Check with your spouse and say, "This is what I'd like to do." It honors your mate to do that. I don't think there's ever been a time when my wife said, "No, you can't do that." But she simply likes to know that she's a valued part of our marriage.

3. Give Freedom in Small Things

A woman actually told me this: "Whenever I have to buy something, my husband drops me off at the store. I go inside and get the exact figure plus tax to the penny. I come out and tell him the amount. He gives me the exact change to the penny. Then I go back inside and purchase the item."

Her husband was sitting there at the time and did not feel he was being demeaning to that woman. He felt he was being holy. And I said to him, "No, you're just dumb. You're dumb because in seeking to control, you're treating your wife like a child. So whatever you think you are gaining, you are actually losing the love of your wife. You need to trust her with things."

Men and women need the freedom to take care of the necessities of life. A woman needs the freedom to run a home. Paul calls a wife the *oikosdespotes*—literally, "the house despot." What a word. It means the manager of the home. She needs to have the freedom to spend some money to do her job.

At the same time, my wife needs to give me the leeway to maintain all of those things that are my responsibility. Even if you have a budget, you still need to show respect to your spouse and give them the freedom to do what they need to do.

4. Women Can Have Money

Most younger folks don't need to hear this, but there are still some people who think women shouldn't make money. But the woman in Proverbs 31 is an extremely gifted businesswoman. She sells belts to the tradesmen. She considers a field and buys it and plants a vineyard from her earnings. As long as husband and wife are in agreement and it doesn't interfere with their marriage, it is good for a woman to pursue her dreams.

5. Decide Who Does the Books

The man does not have to keep track of the money. The wage earner does not have to keep track of the money. In my family, my wife does the books. She does a wonderful job, and I'm happy to let her do it.

Let me give you a bit of guidance on this: if you're the one who does the books, you must do them well. You can't mess up the finances. Your spouse needs to know that things are being done right.

On the flip side, if your mate does the books, then you, in a sense, have to submit yourself to what works best for them. I have to be willing to accept what works best for my wife as she keeps track of our finances. If she needs me to bring in certain receipts and invoices, then I have to do what she thinks is right. I can't use my position as a husband to usurp her authority as the person responsible for the books.

Make life easy for the spouse who keeps track of the finances.

6. Debt Distracts

The whole essence of debt is that you have what you haven't earned. You obligate yourself in the future to pay back the other party with interest. The root word of credit is *credo,* meaning "I believe." They believe that I will pay them back. And the Bible says that the borrower is the lender's slave.

Stay out of debt all that you can because when you take on debt, you give up an equal amount of freedom. You simply can't do some good things because that money is already spoken for. You are obligated to pay back that money.

Some people in our church have gotten themselves into a mess with debt. Often this comes from the assumption that *possessing* equals *living*. They buy into "the word from their sponsor" and purchase stuff, hoping to find happiness and real life. But eventually their joy is taken away by their obligations.

Make whatever choices you have to make to stay out of debt. If you are in debt, do whatever it takes to get out of debt as soon as possible. Are you and your spouse being distracted by debt? Are you on the same page about what you want to do about it?

7. First Things First

Honor the LORD with your wealth,
    with the firstfruits of all your crops;
then your barns will be filled to overflowing,
    and your vats will brim over with new wine.
(Prov. 3:9–10 NIV)

I am amazed how God uses money to make us honor him. That's why Jesus said that your treasure is where your heart is. You can talk all you want about spirituality, but if it doesn't transform your use of money, then your religion is just an intellectual exercise. Money is like lifeblood; it keeps you alive and keeps stuff on your table. God knows how precious it can become to us—that's why he wants the first portion for himself.

Early in my marriage, a friend told me, "Whatever you make, honor God right off the top." My wife and I began doing that. If we had ten dollars, we'd honor God with a buck, and God has always taken care of us. "[H]e who sows sparingly will also reap sparingly, and he who sows bountifully will also reap bountifully. . . . And God is able to make all grace abound to you, so that always having all sufficiency in everything, you may have an abundance for every good deed" (2 Cor. 9:6, 8).

Honor God first. And then always pay what you owe. Pay your bills. And then pay yourself by saving at least 10 percent. And what about the rest? Enjoy it. Have fun with it. Once you honor God, then take care of Caesar and your future, you can enjoy today with the rest of your money. And if you stay out of debt, you have a lot better chance of having better love now in your marriage.

That's why I urge you to ruthlessly keep materialism out of your marriage. It is absolutely opposed to Christianity. It's not following Christ; it's following your lusts. Are there symptoms of the disease of materialism in your marriage?

Both partners need to be on board with this. Whenever I have a discussion time with women, one of the major questions asked is, "What do I do if my husband doesn't want to give to the Lord's work?" That's a tough situation. Should a woman go against her husband and give money behind his back, or should she wait on God while not supporting his work the way she would like?

I answer, "Our church doesn't need your money, but you need to live in harmony. Don't give behind your husband's back; pray and let God fix him." God can fix him really quickly. So if you are a man reading this book, I hope that your wife is not continually being robbed of God's blessing because of your lack of leadership. Don't be a materialistic and self-willed husband. Don't be a materialistic and self-willed wife. Are you both seeking to honor God with your money?

8. Live within Your Income

People get stuck in debt because they want what they can't afford. The only way to have better love now in your marriage is to learn to play the hand you're dealt. The Bible says, "It is He who is giving you power to make wealth" (Deut. 8:18). God deals us different hands. God is not fair. He doesn't deal with everybody the same.

God is good and God is just, but he's not fair. Fair means you always treat everybody in the same manner, and he doesn't. I am a pastor. In America today, there is a certain range of salaries that a pastor makes. I know lots of people who make more money than I do—some of them make a lot more. I have a choice: I can be jealous of all their toys, or I can be thankful for what I have. Every TV commercial, magazine ad, billboard, and Web site is trying to convince you that happiness will come by spending money you don't have. You've got the same choice I have. Choose to live within your income.

I'd like to make a few subpoints here. When you're young and getting married, you don't get to start off where your parents are—they've been working for thirty years. At this point your dad may be pulling down something like $150,000—he is doing really well. What's the average starting salary these days when somebody is young and just married? Maybe $40,000. You have to remember that you can't have all the toys your dad and mom had at $100,000, $80,000, or $150,000. You have to work your way up the system.

I see a lot of young couples who are bitter because they don't have all the toys they used to have back at Momma and Daddy's house. So they start their marriage living beyond their income and quickly sink themselves. Guess who they go running to? Momma and Daddy.

After my son Benjamin got married, he and Amanda lived in Austin. They had an apartment that was converted from a parking garage. It was good for them. "An inheritance gained hurriedly at the beginning / Will not be blessed in the end" (Prov. 20:21). Kids who get too much too quick get messed up.

Second, if you are a wife, don't harangue your husband to make more money than his skills and job level allow. He'll try to do it by working eighty hours a week and will disrupt your family.

The third subpoint is this: if you're a husband, don't make your wife work so you can have more toys. If your wife chooses to work and you all can balance it, that's your privilege; but it is not your wife's obligation. It's a man's obligation to provide. You must work by the sweat of your brow, die young, and give her your insurance. You can't say to your wife, "You have to work." That is not her responsibility.

Many women who are forced into working end up making less than minimum wage when you factor in all the overhead costs to allow them to work (day care, wardrobe, transportation, etc.). I've seen women who are very bitter because they feel they've had to abandon being a wife and mother simply to have toys and to carry on an illusion.

9. Beware a Dual Income

When both the husband and wife work, the couple has an extra income that they might not normally have. But the reality is that nobody wants to make more money; they want to spend more money. So when you have more money, you're automatically going to spend more money. You get accustomed to a lifestyle that depends on both incomes. Then they have their first child, and she decides, "I don't want to put my child in day care and let somebody else raise him. What's the use of having a child if I can't be a mother? I need to quit work." Then her husband looks at the bills and decides she can't quit work because they spend more money than he makes. They've painted themselves into a corner.

So the couple has to make a decision. Is it the kid or the Chrysler? And often the Chrysler wins. I've seen it over and over, and it leads to bitterness and division in marriage. So be careful with double incomes. If both of you work, take the second income and put it aside. Save it for college, retirement, and a rainy day.

10. Enjoy Your Money

Paul said, "Instruct those who are rich in this present world not to be conceited or to fix their hope on the uncertainty of riches, but on God, who richly supplies us with all things to enjoy" (1 Tim. 6:17). Seven times in the book of Ecclesiastes we're told to eat, drink, and be merry. You never let what might happen tomorrow cancel out the happiness of today. Honor God, pay your bills, put some in savings, and enjoy your money.

An old sage in our church said, "Make sure you run out of money and air at the same time." I had a professor at seminary say, "Make sure that your last check bounces." He added, "Preferably to your kid." Enjoy your money. I can show you plenty of verses in the Bible that support going skiing, buying a nice camera, or enjoying a nice outfit. Are you both able to enjoy the life God gives you and the money he provides?

11. Use Your Money for Good

The Bible supports not just enjoying money but using money for good. The apostle Paul said of the righteous man, "HE SCATTERED ABROAD, HE GAVE TO THE POOR, HIS RIGHTEOUSNESS ENDURES FOREVER" (2 Cor. 9:9). Solomon said,

> There is one who scatters, and yet increases all the more,
> And there is one who withholds what is justly due,
> and yet it results only in want.
> The generous man will be prosperous,
> And he who waters will himself be watered.
> (Prov. 11:24–25)

So, like Jesus said, "And I say to you, make friends for yourselves by means of the wealth of unrighteousness, so that when it fails, they will receive you into the eternal dwellings" (Luke 16:9). Doing good with your money can help you establish relationships by which you can share the gospel.

Let me ask you a question. Did you have parents who were conspicuous in their benevolent use of money? If you did, are you glad and proud that you had parents who used their money to help people? That's the testimony you want to give your children. Throw your money at a good cause whenever you see one. God will take care of you. Use your money for good.

12. Honor Your Differences

In many marriages, husbands and wives have different attitudes toward money. If you happen to be a little bit tighter and your spouse a little bit looser, you need to recognize that. If there's a big difference in your attitudes toward money, you need to have a lot of flexibility in your relationship. Don't try to dominate and change the other person on issues that are not sinful. Try to meet in the middle and honor your spouse.

13. Value the Eternal

Jesus said, "The eye is the lamp of your body; when your eye is clear, your whole body also is full of light" (Luke 11:34a). Jesus was saying that how you see things colors the rest of your life. If your values are eternal, then your life will follow in his footsteps, safe and sound in the proper direction. But if your eye is dark and you can't see eternal things, then your whole body is full of darkness and you're going to make some bad decisions.

Is your eye clear? Do you live with the awareness that you are most assuredly going to die one day? There will be no U-Haul parked at your funeral. You're not going to take anything with you. Naked you came into this world, and naked you shall leave.

You'd be surprised how many people live their whole lives as if this weren't true. All the toys you have are not going to bring you any ultimate satisfaction. So if your eye is clear, you'll live for eternal glory, and use money to do good things. This leads to a very useful, happy life.

We have about 1,200 collegians in our evening service at our church, and the place is rocking. A bunch of them have eyes that are clear. They know why they are here—to know God and to make him known. Their dreams are eternal dreams. I look at those young men and women and I just get thrilled. They are going to have the most fun, enjoyable lives because their eyes are clear, and their whole body is going to be full of light. They are going to walk and not stumble. They are going to be living for eternal things, helping them make wise decisions for the rest of life. Chances are, they are going to marry someone with the same values. Together they will find so much significance and have so much fun.

In contrast, whenever I see young men or women with no sense of the eternal, I know that they are going to walk in darkness and make bad decisions. Some of them will succeed in the wrong things, but all of them will end up with a life of pain.

I'm sure you want more for your marriage. How are you doing in the area of money and in your daily life together? Pay attention to the little things that make life pleasant. Allow God to knit your hearts close every day. Keep the heart of the fence post strong, so that you can continue to have better love now.

Chapter 6

What Your Spouse Expects Concerning Life Together

NOBODY COMES INTO MARRIAGE without expectations. Most young men and women have thought quite a bit about what they hope their marriage will be like. A lot of these expectations are unspoken assumptions about how the two of you will live together. Understanding these expectations can help you both get on the same page and continue to deepen your relationship.

How can you have better love now in your daily living? Husband, remember what your wife expected when she heard you say, "I do."

A Wife Expects the Opportunity to Develop

Every woman goes into marriage expecting the opportunity to develop. Even if she couldn't put it into words, she hoped that her union with her husband would help her grow into something greater than she was before.

Husbands, your wife ought to be more because she married you, not less. You don't ever want her thinking, *What could I have been if I had not sidled up to this drone over here? How high could I have risen?*

If you asked your wife today, "Honey, am I helping you become all God wants you to be?" what would she say?

Many married couples are discussed in the Bible. Ananias and Sapphira sure wouldn't be ones we would pick as role models. Mary gets a lot of press, but Joseph fades from the picture pretty quickly. The New Testament really only gives us an extended peek at one couple, Priscilla and Aquila. We read about Priscilla and Aquila on several different occasions.

Aquila means "the eagle." *Priscilla* means "the wise woman." They are always mentioned together. When they are introduced for the first time, it's Aquila and his wife Priscilla (Acts 18:2). The man is mentioned first. This is the common way people are introduced in the Bible: Jacob and Rachel, Isaac and Rebecca, or Abraham and Sarah. And so they are introduced as Aquila and his wife, Priscilla.

But as the narrative goes on, it becomes Priscilla and Aquila (Acts 18:18, 26; Rom. 16:3, etc.). For some reason, Priscilla moves to the forefront. Maybe she was more outgoing. Maybe she was more gifted. Maybe she had more relationships and resources in the community. For whatever reason, she begins to get top billing later on.

Yet when they are first introduced, Aquila is mentioned first. I believe this supports the idea of a woman who is respectful, but also a man who is not intimidated by the talent of his wife. There is never a hint of strife or discord between them. They were pillars in the early church, co-laborers with Paul, who had an impact in many cities. As a man, Aquila helped his wife develop. Instead of being jealous, he helped make her everything she could be.

Consider the woman written about in Proverbs 31. "She considers a field and buys it; / From her earnings she plants a vineyard"

(v. 16). "[She] supplies belts to the tradesmen" (v. 24). "[T]he teaching of kindness is on her tongue" (v. 26). She does a little real estate. She has a textile business and makes some belts. She is a teacher. Yet "she does [her husband] good and not evil / All the days of her life" (v. 12). "Her children rise up and bless her" (v. 28). "Her husband is known in the gates" (v. 23). She doesn't forget her house and family to go pursue some other dream. Her children and her husband receive honor because of her wisdom and skill. And so this woman is everything that she can be.

Men, biblically we also have a husband—Christ. What has he done for you? Has he done you any evil? How has he husbanded you? He has done for you what he does for all his children. He gifts us, encourages us, helps us, and makes us into everything we were created to be.

That's how we ought to think of our wives. "I'm going to take my time, my life, my money, everything I have, and I'm going to help this woman rise as high as she possibly can." Now obviously, a woman should not forget her duties as a wife and mother, but being a great wife and a mother doesn't mean she can't flourish in other ways as well.

My wife has a real talent for teaching small groups. She loves international students. North Texas State University has about 2,000 international students on the campus. And so, on Thursday mornings, my wife loves to take the wives of international students and get them in Bible study. She also gets involved in their lives. She teaches them how to sew. She teaches them how to shop at a supermarket. She helps them learn how to drive and get a license.

As a matter of fact, when we built our house a few years ago, we built a smaller house and added a separate building for these meetings. I was willing to do that because nothing is better than having a happy wife. And there's nothing better than helping your wife become what she is meant to be. When we were deciding the kind of house to build, I wanted to make an investment in her.

Men, the next time you see your wife, I want you to stop and say to yourself, "What has God given me right here? I don't want to be a hindrance to my wife. I want to make her everything she can be." If she likes photography, ask her what kind of camera she needs. Build her a darkroom or buy her some new software for the computer. If she likes gardening, buy her the tools and plants she needs. If she wants to serve on a volunteer board in the community, watch the kids to allow her to make the meetings. Ask your wife about her dreams and then find a way to make them happen.

No woman wants to be trapped in the dead-end drudgery of a humdrum existence that seems to be headed nowhere. Help your wife flourish to the glory of God. Build a life together that helps her become everything God meant for her to be.

A Wife Expects Security

When your wife was standing at the altar and heard you say, "I do," she expected security. She believed she was marrying a man who would always be there. The way you live with your wife on a daily basis needs to increase her security.

I heard a counselor say that, in general, women don't do well with fear. He said, "Men sometimes get bored if life isn't scary. But women like to know that everything is safe and secure." In my experience of working with couples, that rings true most of the time. Men tend to enjoy adventure and risks; women prefer predictability and stability.

A wife doesn't like wondering where her husband is after work. She doesn't like discovering porn on his computer. She doesn't like not knowing why her husband is discouraged or angry or withdrawn. She doesn't like her husband being overly familiar with other women. A wife doesn't do well when she knows that the person who is her partner in life and in her family is on shaky ground.

The woman in the Song of Solomon says to her husband, "Put me like a seal over your heart, / Like a seal on your arm / For love is as strong as death" (8:6). What does it mean that love is as strong as death? Well, death never gives up the people that it claims. When you are dead, you're dead. And she says, "That's the way I am. I'm not going to give you up." So she doesn't want anyone else in her husband's heart.

Sadly, a lot of young women today are being told to make sure they have an escape hatch when they get married. So many women have been left high and dry in the past by men that they are telling young women to protect themselves: "Get a degree and a good job, so if he walks out, you'll be able to make a good life." It sounds like a metaphysical prenuptial agreement, but it is really just planning to fail.

You can certainly understand why women think this way based on the track record of men in America. When a man walks away from a marriage, he often gets another wife and continues on with his life. But what happens if you are a woman who took care of things and didn't work outside the home? What if you didn't get any job training or experience because you were life partners with that man? You were his help, like the Bible says. You worked while he got his education. You managed the household and took care of the kids. Then he went out and got a younger woman. Now you're stuck.

A woman in our church was married to a man who made about a quarter of a million dollars a year. She didn't get her degree. She didn't feel like she needed to. She helped him. And she raised their kids. Then he took off. Now she's on her own. Her income is about $27,500 and she lost everything.

You know what the guy lost? Nothing. But he gained a new, younger wife. Is that fair? A woman doesn't want to feel even a hint that this could happen to her. Husbands, you need to avoid anything that would make your wife feel insecure.

This security is vital for our children as well. As a Christian parent, the first responsibility you have to your child is to create a home that is secure and peaceful. "Better is a dish of vegetables where love is / Than a fattened ox served with hatred" (Prov. 15:17). The Bible says it's better for the dad to make minimum wage, the family to rent an apartment and have to walk everywhere, and have Mom and Dad love each other, than to have a seven-figure income with Mom and Dad hating each other. You simply can't have a Christian home without security.

A friend of mine, Carey Casey, started a ministry in inner-city Chicago. He grew up in an ideal family, and his wife was blessed to come from a good family as well. Carey shared with me that when kids from the inner city came to his house, they would often end up falling asleep. They'd lie down on the staircase, the couch, a chair—almost anywhere—and fall asleep. At first this was puzzling, to say the least.

Then he visited some of their homes. There was so much tension and insecurity where these children lived. There was no order or schedule. In many cases there wasn't a father. Momma was trying to do everything. The kids ran amok. There wasn't any discipline or structure. There was anger and violence. And those kids, as tough as they were, were never able to really relax. They always had to keep their guard up in their own homes.

Then these children would visit Carey's house. There was affection, order, a father who daily gave his life for his family, a wife who respected him, kids who obeyed, cleanliness, music, food, and fun. These children who lived in such inconsistent and difficult home situations came into that safe environment and suddenly felt safe. They were able to actually relax. They could truly rest. And so they fell asleep.

Our children need security in our homes. Husbands, when your wife heard you say, "I do," she expected that you would bring security and stability to your home.

If you don't have peace in your home, anything you teach your children about God will go in one ear and out the other. It will all be just theory. If you aren't living it out, your children will ignore what you say. And if you're really unfortunate, one day they'll be famous and will write a tell-all memoir about their hypocritical parents.

I have had parents in my church who are very strict. They cross every *t* and dot every *i* in child-rearing. They don't allow any kind of entertainment or any music with a beat. Their idea of the latest musical fad is Gregorian chants. Yet, in some cases, these homes are filled with strife because the husband is so dishonoring to his wife, and she is so impertinent to him. There is no affection. There's no love, no tenderness, and no security. They think the standard of child-rearing is forbidding fun things to do.

Your wife isn't the only one who expected security in your marriage—your children need it too. If you want better love now, you need to hug each other, kiss each other, be committed to each other, and build a home that is safe and secure. (You could also let your kids boogie just a little bit without worrying about it, but that's another book.)

I remember very well a conversation I had at a Song of Solomon conference several years ago. A woman came up to me, and with great pride she said, "When my husband asked me to marry him, we went to the city square and bought our rings, then we went straight to the cemetery and bought our burial plots." She deserved to say it with great pride. "We buy our rings, and then we buy our burial plots because we are committed to each other until death." That's old-school marriage, right there, and she was proud of it.

A Wife Expects Affection

If you want better love now, you also need to realize that when your wife heard you say, "I do," she also expected affection. By *affection* I am primarily referring to nonsexual touching. In some cases a man may naturally seek and give affection more than his wife, but usually a man needs to adjust to his wife's needs for affection. Too often men use affection as a bribe or a down payment, hoping that sex will follow. True affection has no strings attached. Whether touching her hand, putting an arm around her shoulder, or brushing the hair from her cheek, you are communicating, "I love you because you are you." It's love with skin on it—touching somebody and letting them know that they're precious to you.

I heard a great quote from a lady in my church. She told one of the women in our office, "I wish my body parts were put on with Velcro so I could take them off, put them in a box, give them to my husband, and say, 'Here, go play with them.'"

Women just love to be groped by their husbands—it's right up there at the top of their wish list. That's why some wives are afraid to do the dishes with their husband in the kitchen because they have to turn their backs on them. Maybe you were wondering why your wife put that little mirror by the kitchen sink? She wants to get the jump on you.

Affection is communicated through nonsexual touching. My wife is not an overly affectionate person, but when we pray together at night, I put her head on my shoulder. I'll just rub her hair and gently scratch her head while we pray.

People receive affection in different ways. Some enjoy touch; others like acts of service. Others appreciate encouraging words or gifts and remembering special occasions. And some like quality time together. Guys, learn how your wife receives affection and play the hand you're dealt.

My son, a former military sniper and now a federal agent, is not all that into hugging. But when he saw the woman who is now his wife, he said, "I've got to have this girl." And he went after her. He drove 400 miles one time just to surprise her with her favorite ice cream. One time he covered the house with candles, cooked for her, and gave her twelve handpicked roses. He put a love note or a gift in each rose, and as the blooms opened over the next few days, each revealed its gift. After that gesture I said, "Son, that ain't bad, but that's some kind of encore you're going to have to come up with."

He's about six foot three. His precious wife is about five feet tall and weighs maybe 100 pounds. She is very affectionate and loves to put her arms around him when he's sitting in a chair. One day when she wrapped him in a big hug from behind, he said, "Eeee-www," and made a nasty face. My wife took him aside and said, "Let me tell you something," and his ears pricked up. She said, "When your wife does that to you publicly, it's not because she wants a hug. She's making a statement to all the watching world that 'this is my man.' If you make that silly face, you're saying, 'This is not my girl.' You better melt in her arms when she holds you like that." Then she took out a gun and pistol-whipped him. OK, just kidding about that last part.

Men, show affection to your wives.

It's not just women who have expectations about what life will be like after they are married. If you are going to have better love now in your life together, there are some things that husbands expect when they hear their wives say, "I do."

A Husband Expects the Freedom to Minister

When a man is standing at the altar and hears his mate say, "I do," one of the things he thinks that means is that in his daily life he will have the freedom to minister. With all the struggles a man has with the world, the flesh, and the devil, he doesn't want to feel like he has to drag his wife around in order to be godly. He doesn't want to feel like every service opportunity is a battle.

In 1 Corinthians 7, Paul works through the marital issues going on in the Corinthian church. One of their questions was, "Should you stay single and serve God fully, or should you be married?" So in verses 25 and 26, Paul says, "Now concerning virgins I have no command of the Lord, . . ." [this meant that Jesus did not explicitly teach anything concerning singleness] ". . . but I give an opinion as one who by the mercy of the Lord is trustworthy. I think then that this is good in view of the present distress, that it is good for a man to remain as he is." Paul says that in this persecuting world it is easier to serve God as a single. Most people can't do this.

So Paul goes on to say in verse 27, "Are you bound to a wife? Do not seek to be released." Divorce is not an option once one is married. He continues: "Are you released from a wife?"—meaning that your wife has divorced you—"Do not seek a wife." Stay single. "But if you marry, you have not sinned; and if a virgin marries, she has not sinned" (v. 28a)—meaning, the virgin who marries and the abandoned divorcee who remarries have not sinned. He speaks very honestly. Single people are always coming to me and asking, "What did Paul mean in that verse?" And I say, "Paul meant just what he said." He says in verse 28b, "Yet such will have trouble in this life, and I am trying to spare you."

If you were to do a postdoctoral analysis of the Greek word for trouble that Paul uses in this passage by studying original manuscripts and cross-referencing them against other occurrences of this word in the ancient world, you'll discover that Paul means . . . *trouble.* He meant exactly what he said. That's marriage. When you get married, there is going to be trouble. That's a fact.

When I teach this at a singles' conference, people always come up to me and say, "Really?" Yeah, there's trouble. If you get married, you will have to apologize. You have to submit your will to someone else's. You have to be selfless for the good of your spouse. And then kids come along and magnify all of this exponentially. Add to the relational issues the financial struggles. Can two live together as cheaply as one? Sure, if one goes naked and the other starves. So marriage brings all kinds of difficulty.

Paul says, "I am trying to spare you." In verse 29 he says, "[T]his I say, brethren, the time has been shortened, so that from now on those who have wives should be as though they had none; and those who weep, as though they did not weep; and those who rejoice, as though they did not rejoice; and those who buy, as though they did not possess." This verse needs to be interpreted correctly. Paul is saying that whether you are up or down right now, don't get too uptight about it because the Lord is going to return and make all things new.

Did you get a new car, a new dress, or a new house? Enjoy it, but don't get too hopped up over it because the time is short. Christ is coming. Don't get too excited about the things you own because Christ is coming. The kingdoms of this world will become the kingdoms of our Lord and Christ. We're going to lose everything. Paul instructs us "to be free from concern" (1 Cor. 7:32). That's what he means when he says to live as if you didn't have a spouse. We can't allow marriage to change our philosophy of life as a Christian.

When I was a single man and came to know Christ, all I wanted was to stew on God. I thought I had discovered something new to Western man. I didn't know if anybody else knew about this God stuff but me and the guy who shared the gospel with me. I was amazed that I could know God and walk with him. I immersed myself in the things of God. I couldn't believe that when I preached the gospel, people came to faith. I could invest my life in eternity.

Like most men, I have always looked for something to die for. I just couldn't find anything worth my life. When I became a Christian, I found it. I wanted to serve God.

Then I went to a Campus Crusade meeting and ran into this girl who had the same commitment I did. She wanted to serve God. And so I got in my lane on the track, and she got in her lane on the track, and it turned out we were running side by side. I saw this happening and said, "Let's run together." And that's how we got married. We had a common commitment to God that was stronger than our commitment to one another.

What was Eve's job in the book of Genesis? She wasn't there to distract Adam from his calling. She was a helper suitable for Adam while he cultivated, subdued, and multiplied. Their relationship wasn't supposed to bring conflict but to help them both fulfill the calling God had given.

So I said to my wife-to-be, "You don't have to worry about being a missionary and raising support now. You've got a one-man support board. I'll be your pack mule. I'm going to take care of you. And I don't have to worry about botulism and salmonella because I've got you. And I don't have to suffer from a twenty-four-hour virus or live in squalor anymore. We can take care of each other." We help each other attain our common goal of serving God. I'm not going to distract her; she's not going to distract me. That's the way it's meant to be—like Priscilla and Aquila, serving God together.

Near the end of his ministry, Paul says, "Greet Prisca and Aquila, my fellow workers in Christ Jesus, who for my life risked their own necks, to whom not only do I give thanks, but also all the churches of the Gentiles" (Rom. 16:3–4). This couple risked everything for Paul and the gospel. They didn't play it safe because they were married. Marriage is not supposed to take you away from your common purpose. So often a committed Christian guy and a committed Christian girl get married, and together they form a disgustingly lukewarm couple. First they have kids, then focus on sports, then college money becomes a big issue. Bit by bit, knowing and serving God passionately becomes just a distant memory of what it was like in college.

One of the guys I discipled came back depressed from a college reunion. He said, "When I was in college with my Christian friends and we were all single, we used to dream about God, ministry, China, and Africa. We wanted to live for great things. Now that we are all married, it seems that we are weighed down by a desire to maintain our families and physical lives."

"Those who have wives should be as though they had none." Marriage is not meant to distract you. Think about what it's like when a single man needs to move from one city to another. He opens up a bed sheet, puts all his stuff in it, and drags it to the car. When you're married, it takes Bekins and Mayflower with five moving guys because we collect all kinds of stuff. Marriage can be a tool Satan uses to tame you and make you worldly. You can lose your radical commitment.

Is that the will of God? Should ministry be done only by single people until they get married and become compromised married people? My wife and I fight this. In marriage, it seems you're covered with Velcro and there's all kinds of junk that attaches to you. There's a "tyranny of the urgent" of things you have to do. You have to force yourself to travel light as a couple. That's why Paul says if you get married, you're going to have trouble. So if you can stay single, stay single.

And if you are married, fight complacency and compromise. C. T. Studd was a British missionary to China in the late 1800s. When he turned twenty-five, he inherited a large sum of money from his father. Through prayer, C. T. felt led to give his entire fortune to Christ. Before knowing the exact amount of his inheritance, C. T. gave away £25,000. When he learned the actual total of his inheritance, he had about £3,400 remaining.

Shortly thereafter, C. T. married a young Irish missionary named Priscilla Stewart. Just before the wedding, he presented his bride with the remaining money. She said, "Charlie, what did the Lord tell the rich young man to do?"

"Sell all."

"Well then, we will start clear with the Lord at our wedding."

And they gave the rest of the money away.[5] Some of it went to a fledgling institution in the United States, the Moody Bible Institute. That's a wife who supports her husband in his calling.

Recognize the unique expectations that each person brings to your marriage and your life together. Keep the fence post strong, and God can use your marriage to help both of you become all he meant you to be, for his glory.

Keeping the Fence Post Solid

Key Concepts about Your Life Together

- Marriage is relentless in its togetherness.
- It's all "our money" because the two have become one flesh.
- Give freedom in small things but agree on major expenditures.
- Support the person who does the books.
- Live within a single income, so you don't depend on both spouses working.
- A wife expects the opportunity to develop.
- A wife expects security.
- A wife expects affection.
- A husband expects the freedom to minister.

Straightening the Post

Discussion for Better Love Now

1. How do couples you know struggle in their life together? Do you see any of these struggles in your relationship?

2. How well do you and your mate deal with money? Which of the principles given in chapter 5 will help your marriage the most?

3. Which of the expectations for a wife do you think needs the most work in your marriage (the opportunity to develop, security, and affection)? What about the expectations of a husband (the freedom to minister)?

4. What is the most important thing God might want you to do differently in the next week to see a change in your life together? What is one concrete step you could take to make that change?

Fence Post 4: Family Life

When you got married, you may have thought that you were marrying your spouse-to-be. That's actually not true. You were marrying your spouse-to-be and their family. When you marry someone, a whole bunch of other people come along too.

Family is a huge part of having better love now. When you have siblings and parents and eventually children, things can get complicated quickly. Getting relationships right within your family is a vital key to having better love now.

The next two chapters will help you evaluate how you are doing as a family. But first, have a short discussion to discover how you both think you're doing now in your family life.

Rate your marriage in the area of family. As with the previous sections, my goal is to get you thinking about each area before you read what I've written and what the Bible says. Have a short, ten-minute discussion with your spouse to prepare you for what God might want to do in your heart.

Fence Post 4: Family Life

Wife's Perspective

How would you rate your marriage in the area of your family? Use the following to chart your thoughts.

With a pencil, draw a line on each fence post to show your rating for your marriage in the area of your family.

Our relationships are all right on track.

We take the fun out of dysfunctional.

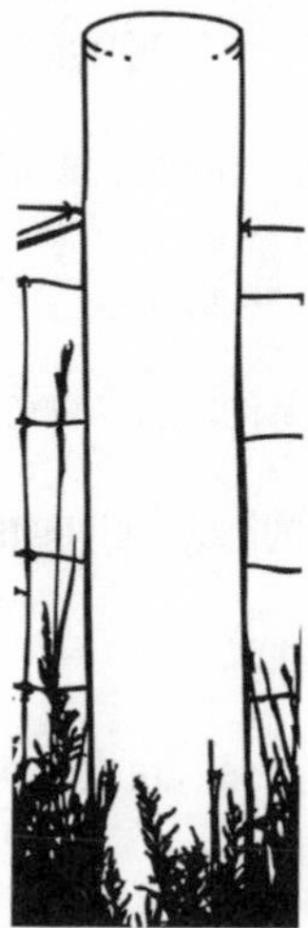

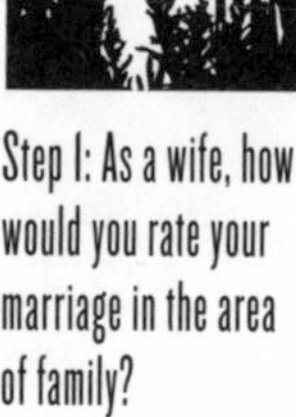

Step 1: As a wife, how would you rate your marriage in the area of family?

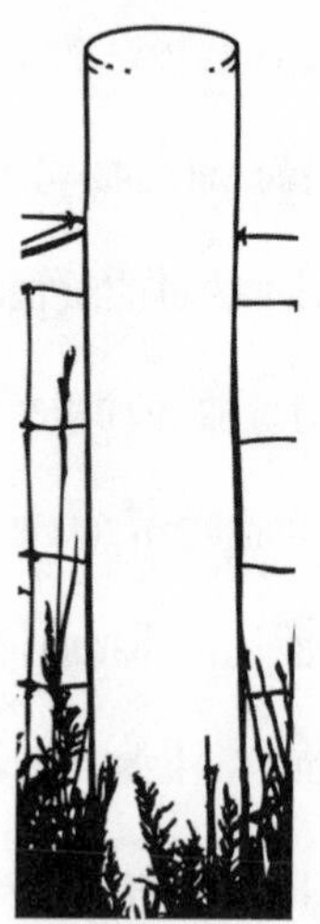

Step 2: How will your husband rate your marriage in the area of family?

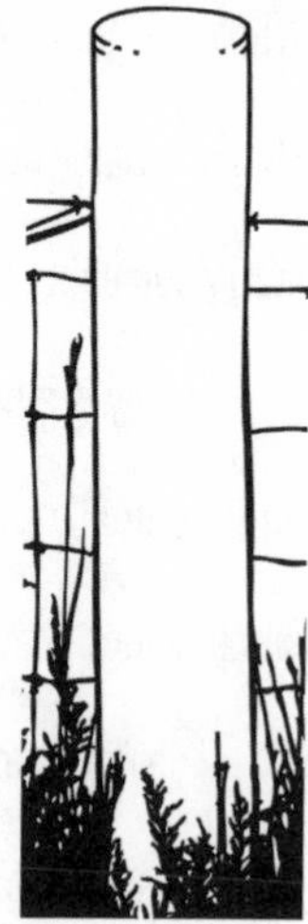

Step 3: What will your husband say you thought? Mark where he will say you rated your marriage in the area of family.

Fence Post 4: Family Life

Husband's Perspective

As a husband, how would you rate your marriage in the area of family? Use the following to chart your thoughts.

With a pencil, draw a line on each fence post to show your rating in the area of your family.

Our relationships are all right on track.

We take the fun out of dysfunctional.

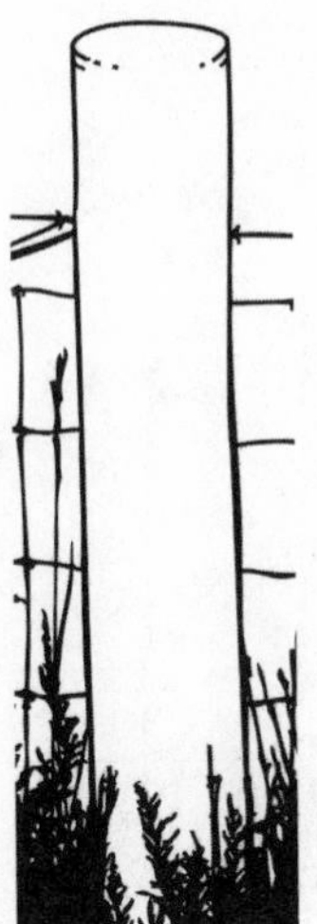

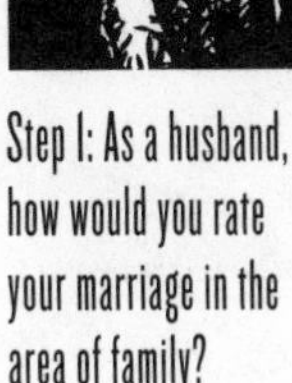

Step 1: As a husband, how would you rate your marriage in the area of family?

Step 2: How will your wife rate your marriage in the area of family?

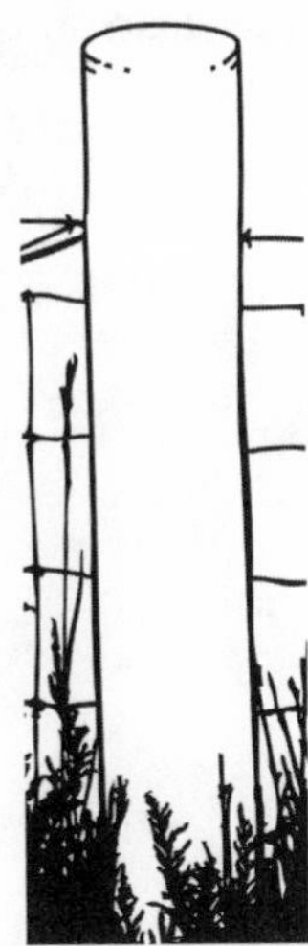

Step 3: What will your wife say you thought? Mark where she will say you rated your marriage in the area of family.

For Discussion:

Take about ten minutes and work your way from step 1 to step 3. For each step, share why you rated your family life the way you did. (Note that the wife's step 3 corresponds to the husband's step 2.)

What issues does this raise that you want to consider more deeply? Are there areas in which you and your spouse have a different perspective? Have you seen some potential areas of conflict that need to be addressed?

Have a short prayer, asking God to help you both change in any ways necessary to have better love now.

Now read the chapters and talk through the discussion and application questions at the end.

Chapter 7

Family Relationships

MARRIAGE DOESN'T HAPPEN IN a vacuum. A man is a son before he is a husband. A woman is a daughter before she is a wife. After marriage, many couples eventually have children. The husband has friends. The wife has friends. And every couple has friends together.

These relationships form a web that is interconnected. You can't pull on one strand of the web without affecting the other parts. The family is an interdependent system. It functions well and has a positive impact on its members, or it functions poorly and is destructive.

You've seen families where a particularly difficult person seemed to rip the family apart. It may have been a teenage son or daughter or perhaps a father-in-law or mother-in-law. But this person becomes the focal point of all the efforts of the family. The other relationships within the family shift and change as different members take on roles they think will help the family cope. Soon the family relationships are so far out of balance that the situation feels hopeless.

Bill and Sally in our church have four children. Three of them were model children. Their firstborn, however, decided to commandeer the family. She rebelled in every way known to man and probably invented a few new ways too. Often, her parents felt like they had to give in to her just to bring some sanity to their lives. That seemed to be the only way the other kids could have any peace. Finally, they gave her an ultimatum and a ticket to a youth home. But she still had destroyed every other relationship in the family.

I've counseled plenty of couples who were in situations much like this. I've got to admit, it's pretty discouraging. I want to tell them to turn back the clock five or ten years and nip some of these things in the bud. I want to make it all better by saying a prayer or having an intervention or sending someone to boot camp. Unfortunately, it's almost never that easy.

A marriage is always more than just the relationship between a woman and a man. If the rest of your relationships don't work, your marriage won't work. If you want to have better love now, you need to make sure the heart of your family life remains strong.

The Family in God's Plan

Solomon, who saw family problems firsthand, said it best about the importance of family. He tied the success of the family into the success of a nation and the world. "Unless the Lord builds the house, they labor in vain who build it; unless the Lord guards the city, the watchman keeps awake in vain" (Ps. 127:1). In short, without God as the basis of the nation, the nation's efforts will ultimately be futile.

Then Solomon says, "Behold, children are a gift of the Lord, the fruit of the womb is a reward" (Ps. 127:3). The family, which is the foundation of any nation, must be recognized as being from

God also. A nation who does not honor God in the home will never honor him in the streets and the market. The biblical picture is Christ over Daddy, who's over Mommy, who with her husband is over the kids—all things done in order.

The family is at the heart of God's plan for the world. It's the earliest institution God ordained (Gen. 2), and it's his primary means for passing the faith on to future generations (Ps. 78). One key to having better love now is making sure you and your spouse are on the same page regarding your family.

In the next chapter, we'll again focus on expectations of husbands and wives. But in this chapter we'll deal with some common struggles both husbands and wives have with family.

I've found that dealing with in-laws is one of the top five issues that married men and women face, but if you attend church regularly, you've probably never heard a sermon on your relationship with your in-laws. I'm not sure I've ever talked to a pastor who has preached a sermon on in-laws. I preached one sermon on this topic, and it happened to fall during the Christmas season. At the time, I joked with my congregation that I was absolutely confident we had the full attention of the Holy Spirit at the church. Nowhere else in the world was any pastor preaching on marriage and in-laws that Sunday. Not only that, but it actually fell on December 7, Pearl Harbor Day. Somehow it seemed appropriate.

When you get married, you pick up a set of parents and don't have any choice about whether to keep them. And if you're a father or a mother and your child gets married, you pick up a child in a hurry. Either way, pretty soon these new family members are right in the middle of your life—they even show up at your breakfast table.

In this chapter we're going to focus on how a young married couple should relate to their new parents. (For those with married children, I've added an appendix to help you relate to your new child.)

Here are five rules of engagement for relating to these new parents.

1. Honor Your In-Laws

One of the most famous verses in the Bible is Ruth 1:16—"Where you go I will go, and where you stay I will stay. Your people will be my people and your God my God" (NIV). We quote that quite often in weddings as if it were a statement from a wife to a husband. But in the original context of the book of Ruth, these words were not spoken by a wife to a husband but by a daughter-in-law to her mother-in-law. The Bible demonstrates that we should honor our new parents.

One practical application: avoid criticizing your spouse's parents. When you do, you are forcing your spouse into a very awkward position—they either agree with you or defend their parents. (If your spouse points out a few things that bug them about their parents, feel free to add a soft "amen," but don't initiate the conversation.)

In 1 Timothy 5, we see that the command to honor your parents still holds when you get married, even if they are your spouse's parents. Paul takes seriously the church's role in helping elderly people. He says, "Honor widows who are widows indeed" (v. 3). In verse 17, we see that honoring carries with it the idea of financial support: "The elders who rule well are to be considered worthy of double honor." Thus, to honor the widow is to financially look to her needs. James 1:27a says, "Pure and undefiled religion . . . is this: to visit orphans and widows in their distress." That word *visit* comes from a word that means "to oversee, to look out for their needs."

But in 1 Timothy 5:4 there is a certain widow that the church is not supposed to take care of because someone else has that responsibility: "But if a widow has children or grandchildren, these should learn first of all to put their religion into practice by caring for their own family and so repaying their parents and grandparents, for this is pleasing to God" (NIV). Paul is saying that when we get older, you and I have a responsibility to pay back our parents.

As folks are living longer and longer, many more children are experiencing a time of reversal as their parents age. In many ways children are having to parent their parents. We should not look to the government to take care of them. Even if they have Social Security, that's just added money if they need it. And we should not look to the church to take care of them.

According to this text, children and grandchildren have the responsibility to take care of aging parents. My brothers and I told our mother as she got older, "Don't worry. Whatever you need, we'll take care of it. If you want to move from Waco to live with us, you can. If you want your own house here, we'll find a way. If you want your own room, anything you need, we're going to take care of you."

This doesn't apply only to your parents; it also applies to your in-laws. That's why I tell young people when they get married, "You need to discuss this with your spouse. You're going to have a responsibility someday, so you need to be wise and prepare financially to take care of both sets of parents."

Paul goes on to say, "If anyone does not provide for his own, and especially those of his household, he has denied the faith and is worse than an unbeliever" (1 Tim. 5:8). If even pagans naturally know they should care for their parents, how much more should the Christian? So the first rule? Don't run down your mate's parents; instead, honor them and care for them.

2. Leave Your Parents

"For this reason a man shall leave his father and his mother, and be joined to his wife; and they shall become one flesh" (Gen. 2:24). When you get married, a new family has been initiated. There's a sense that you are leaving your parents. You still honor your parents, but there is a different order or priority. In the book of Numbers, the vow made by a young girl wasn't binding unless her father said it was OK. A young girl's faith and devotion could never usurp the order of the home. The father could OK it, or the father could negate it. Once that woman got married, Numbers 30 shows that if she decided to make a vow, the father's consent is not even mentioned. The father is not a controlling element in that girl's life anymore. Can he give counsel? Yes. Can he give asked-for advice? Yes. Should he be a model? We hope. But now the husband is the one who has to consent to the vow. So there is an expected changeover of priorities when two people get married.

Here's a practical application: don't talk to your parents more than you talk to your spouse. A wife who calls home to talk to mother every day is probably asking for trouble. (Don't let things go to the other extreme—my wife frequently gets after me and says, "Would you call your mother?") You have to transition from that intimate bond with your parents, so it won't become an intrusive thing in your home. You have to break it. You not only don't call home every day; you also don't run home at the first sign of trouble.

Of course there are occasions when things get out of hand and your personal safety is at stake. We have had at least two occasions in our church where fathers have had to take their daughters out of their homes because of abuse. But normally speaking, you don't run home as soon as problems start; you work through them together if at all possible.

You also don't look to your parents when you are in need. If finances start getting short, don't have your parents' number on speed dial like you did in high school and college. Don't look to Mommy and Daddy to bail you out. Have I ever helped out my married sons? Sure, I've helped them, when I saw a need or opportunity and asked if I could help. But if one of them were calling every month, that would not be good or healthy for his marriage. You need to leave your father and mother.

How are you doing on leaving your parents? Would you say you have an appropriate relationship that reflects your status as a married couple?

3. Confront Your Own Parents

Whenever there is an issue that needs to be dealt with, the natural-born child should deal with their own parent. It's awkward for any child to confront their parents about a difficult issue; it's more awkward for the in-law to step in.

The son- or daughter-in-law should join in only as a last resort because such a step will be particularly difficult for the parents to accept. Often it can burn bridges. But there are some times that it has to happen. There are some parents who, if they are not confronted, will ruin a marriage. And sometimes that bridge has to be burned. It sounds terrible, but it has to be.

I saw this happen with a young woman's mother. She continually harangued and criticized her daughter. She hurt her feelings, embarrassed her, and made her cry. That old woman had this girl so far under her thumb that her daughter was afraid to speak up. After counseling them and getting the full story, I told her husband, "It's time for you to step in and assure your mother-in-law that she is not going to do that to your wife ever again. And if she does, she will not be coming to your home. She will not be playing with her grandchildren. You will sever her tie for the good of your marriage and your family." He stepped in there and fixed it. But that is definitely the worst-case scenario for extreme circumstances that cannot be handled any other way.

In normal situations, the natural-born child needs to go to Momma and Daddy and say, "Please, I think you need to back off a little bit." Hopefully that won't happen, but that's how to handle it if it does.

Fortunately, I'm not giving this message out of personal experience. My wife would kill me if I didn't clarify this in the book. I have wonderful in-laws. I could wish my in-laws on all of you. They have become my parents and have loved me well.

4. Don't Withdraw from Your Family

Often I will hear of children who get married and don't want to go home again because they think they have to sever their relationship with their parents. That's wrong. One of the biggest problems in American life is that we have lost the idea of our extended family.

I don't know about you, but I grew up with grandparents. I could go from my house on Wind Street over to Reuter Avenue and find my grandfather and grandmother. I could go farther on to North Nineteenth and find my paternal grandfather. They were part of our lives as a family. As a little boy, I grew up with the veneration of my grandfather and my grandmother. They reinforced proper conduct. If I was getting ornery, all my grandfather had to do was clear his throat.

Did you ever experience that? If you didn't, you missed out. I never wanted Grandpa to reprove me. I was in awe of my grandparents. They were the people my parents revered. I also grew up with uncles, aunts, nephews, nieces, and cousins. It was *wonderful*. They were my parents' allies. They all worked together to help raise me to be the man I am today.

Don't eliminate the greatest ally you have in raising your children—your parents. Teresa and I glory in the times that we get to build into our grandchildren. Many of you reading this book live a long way from your parents. Make the effort to keep them involved. Are you connecting with your parents in appropriate ways, so they can contribute to raising your children?

5. Accept Advice from Your Parents

If your mother remembers something she did wrong in 1971 and sees you doing it the same way now, you'd be smart to let her help you out. Granted, there is a way to give advice and a way not to. But if your father calls you over to the side and says, "Son, you can't do that. I tried it, and you can't do it," you ought to listen.

My brother Bobby had been married just a few months when we all went down to our mother's for Christmas. After a day or so, my mother noticed something in the way my brother was addressing his wife. I knew something was up because Momma turned to Bobby and said, "Bobby, let's go get a loaf of bread." And Bobby unwittingly said, "Sure, Mom." I found out later that during the trip, Momma had told Bobby, "Pull over. We need to discuss something."

My brother was wise enough to accept her advice. He had never been a husband before, so when my mother said, "Let me tell you how Nellie feels when you speak that way," he took the reproof. We all need help when we are young and amateurs. Don't buck when your parents step in; they still have their role in your life. The Fifth Commandment doesn't get rescinded at the altar. You still need to honor your parents, and they will have a contribution to make in your life until they pass on to heaven.

Having a right relationship with your parents and in-laws will be one of the greatest blessings for your marriage. Having a bad relationship will be a curse that will drag you down over and over again. Do whatever it takes to make these extended relationships right for the sake of your marriage and better love now.

Chapter 8

What Your Spouse Expects about Your Family Life

All of us enter marriage with expectations about our family. We have ideas and dreams, some of which we have treasured for years. These expectations can be extremely powerful. If you want to have better love now, there are certain things you will need to square away in your family.

Let's start with a wife's expectations about family life.

A Wife Wants a Husband She Can Trust with Her Children

One of the things a woman expects when she hears her husband say, "I do," is that she will have pride in her husband. She wants a husband who has integrity. She wants a husband she can depend on and trust, especially when it comes to her family.

Women are innately concerned about things affecting their children. They want to know that all the people and things influencing their children are having a positive impact. They care about the forces that shape their children's worldview. And a woman knows that no force is more powerful than a father. She wants a husband who is going to provide a good model for their kids.

What's interesting about this is that this desire is not always evident to the woman before she gets married. In the same way, a lot of women are attracted to happy-go-lucky "Peter Pan" men, many young women are also attracted to "rogue–males," who are rough, self-reliant, and aggressive men. They are impressive. They feel dangerous. After they get married, these men are very interested in having their wives submit to them. But they don't feel the need to submit to anybody themselves.

I have two sons and no daughters. But if I had a daughter and a man came to me who wanted to spend time with her, I—knowing men the way I do—would have a conversation with him. I would say, "Young man, for some reason, my daughter likes you. And that's good. Maybe this can go somewhere, and if it does, you are going to want my daughter to follow you. Young man, let me ask you a question: who do you follow? You are going to want her to submit to you, but who do you submit to?" And I would ask that young man, "When did you bow your knee to the Son of God?"

A man cannot be a husband until he's been a bride. Men must submit to Christ before they can learn to lead a wife. Until you learn to follow, you can't lead because men who don't know how to follow either become irresponsible or abusive. They are either passive and ignore their roles as leaders, or they carry around an iron pipe and demand their way all the time.

These men don't know how to lay their lives down. If I were interviewing a young man for my daughter, I would ask him what he read in his Bible today. (Then I would probably ask him to quote his favorite verse from the book of Habakkuk. Maybe that's why God didn't give me any daughters.)

When a woman says, "I do," she wants a husband who can be a model for her children. Sometimes women get attracted to these rogue males: the drinker, the partier, the hell-raiser. These men are on the inside track of a perverse society that honors the wrong things, so they often end up being popular. They attract attention. They seem like fun. There is a lot of competition for their affection. Many women are attracted to these types of men, and some women end up marrying one.

But once a woman gets married, that rogue-male stuff doesn't work so well. Consider a woman who bonds with a guy because both of them have a hatred of authority. Then they get married. What do you think happens to that rebellious girl? She needs bread on the table and a roof over her head. Pretty soon they have children and she starts loving them. And that same girl who married that hell-raising guy, you know what she wants now? She wants a seventeenth-century Puritan. She wants a man who will lead her in worship, pray over their food, take them to church, and teach Bible stories to her children.

And so, that rebel boy who was such a thrill isn't so cute after you get married. A woman wants to have a sense of pride in her husband. She wants to know that she won't have to protect their children from their father. She doesn't want to say to her children, "I know you hear that language from your father, but you're not going to say it." How can she say to her six-year-old son, "Please differentiate between the things that are noble and true and the inappropriate behavior of your father that you witness on a daily basis"? That's asking a child to think with the acumen of a Cambridge scholar.

So a wife doesn't want to feel her children are being jeopardized by the conduct of their father.

We have words for just this situation—when a person says one thing and does another—*duplicity* and *hypocrisy*. The opposite of these is *integrity*. The word *integrate* means "oneness." Something that is integral comes together as a whole. A woman instinctively wants that from her husband: "I want a man who holds to something and lives in agreement with it so I can turn to my children and say, 'Follow this man.'"

My daughter-in-law, the wife of my younger son, sent me a letter for Father's Day. It said, "I want you to know something. John is as good a husband as I could have ever dreamed. He is kind to me. He listens to me. When I go off and say crazy things, he is there to be patient with me and love me. He's the leader in my home; he's strong, but he's tender. I asked John last week, 'How did you get to be such a good husband?' And he said, 'I just followed Pops.' He said, 'Daddy did it and I want to do it too.'"

That letter is now framed in my house. That's how much it means.

Men, are you acting with integrity toward your children? Do you want your sons and daughters to turn out like you? Perhaps more important, does your wife want your sons and daughters to turn out like you? If you want better love now, invest in your kids in a way that will help your wife be thankful for your role in their lives.

A man also had expectations for his family when he got married. If you want to have better love now, wives need to understand their husband's hopes and dreams.

A Husband Wants a Mother for His Children

When a man hears his wife say, "I do," at the altar, he expects that she will be a good mother for his children. He wants to marry a woman who will help him raise godly children.

First Timothy 2 is the controversial chapter where Paul describes the role of men and women in the church. He describes a man's role in chapter 3, but in chapter 2, verse 12, he makes it clear that a woman's purpose is not to lead the church: "But I do not allow a woman to teach or exercise authority over a man, but to remain quiet." Does that mean a woman has a lesser purpose than a man? Paul settles that in verse 15 ("women will be preserved through the bearing of children if they continue in faith and love and sanctity with self-restraint"). Paul is saying that a woman's purpose is not to rule men; it is to raise them. Mothers are an integral part of God's plan for the family as an institution of faith and grace.

If we were to ask one hundred readers of this book, "Were you led to faith by your mother?" a vast majority of them would say yes. Mothers shape the hearts and minds of their children in a way that is different than fathers.

When I was working on the content of this book, my wife was making big flannel boards to teach our grandchildren. People ask me at times, "What does your wife do?" Sometimes I say, "She gives life to eternal humanity and raises them in the image of God. What does yours do?" Mothers often bring children to faith. No matter what else a woman does, no matter where else a woman serves, there will never be any higher calling than shaping a human life. That is a woman's greatest purpose. That's why Paul says in Titus 2:4 that women are to love their husbands and to love their children.

When you see a close-up of a player at a sporting event, what does he always say? "Hi, Mom!" I'm sure my son will do it, too, if he ever gets in a game for the St. Louis Cardinals. Will it matter that I hit 50 million ground balls to him while he was growing up? No. Will it matter that I threw the baseball with him until after dusk, when all I could see was a white blur zooming toward my face? No. Will I be laughed at by my buddies in public because my son forgets I exist? Yes. Is it right? No, it's not right. But what will he say? "Hi, Mom!"

He'll say it because Momma took care of him from his earliest memory. There is a metaphysical umbilical cord between a child and mother that is still attached throughout their lives.

My mother was LaVelle Perry Nelson. If she had been a man, she would have been Douglas MacArthur. She took all four of us boys and said, "You're going to go to college. We're going to find your talent and we're going to shape it." My mother developed us. She would not tolerate anything but our best. I don't care if we were mowing the lawn. My father taught us how to laugh, but my mother shaped our lives. We all revere and honor her.

I remember when I was a sophomore in high school. I started for the varsity baseball team at Waco Richfield High School in Waco, Texas. No sophomore had ever started for the varsity. Before the first game, my mother came to me and said, "Are you ready?" I was kind of hanging my head and said, "These guys are big." They were eighteen and done with puberty, and I hadn't even begun to pubert.

My mother said, "What are you afraid of?"

"Oh, I've never played with guys like this."

She said, "Come out in the backyard."

We went out in the backyard, and she stood me next to our cedar fence. She gave me my baseball glove. Now, my mother played violin for the Waco Symphony. She was not some big athlete. I had no idea what she was going to do. But she took a baseball bat and a ball and stood about fifteen feet from me. And she said, "Here, catch this." And I thought, *What's this crazy woman going to do?* She held that baseball bat like a tennis racket and—*boom!*—she started beating me to death with baseballs. I caught them left and right. After five or ten minutes, she said, "See, you can catch anything that comes your way."

We played against Killeen, Texas, the next day. This story sounds almost too good to be true, but it's the honest truth. I was starting at shortstop. Their first batter was a big, old Texas boy. Our pitcher hung a lazy curve, and the batter just turned on it. He hit a rope of a line drive off to my right, and, out of instinct, I laid out with everything I had. I can still see that ball hanging in the web of my glove. The first pitch of my high-school career, and I made a diving catch. The whole stands came to their feet. I looked up, and my mother was about to burst with pride.

All four of us went to college and all four of us got scholarships. Two of the scholarships were in music and two were in sports. My mother took what we had and developed us. She gave all of us esteem. When my brother played a part in an operetta, we all dressed up in our coats and ties and went to listen to my brother. Whenever my brother Jimmy played a baseball game for Hardin Simmons University, we were there. When I was playing quarterback, she was there. It didn't matter what we did. We were to do it well. She gave us all a sense of purpose. That was my mother.

No matter what else happens in my life, I will always go back to the fountain from which I came. She was the shaper of my life. Every man wants to know his children are going to be cared for by a woman like that.

A Husband Wants a Wife First and a Mother Second

At the same time, men expect their wives to keep them as their top priority above their children. In many families today, children have become idols and an object of worship. Everything the family does revolves around the children—their schedules, their interests, their desires.

In these families, it's easy for moms to become more emotionally connected to their children than they are to their husbands. They spend more time with the kids and talk more with their kids—especially their daughters—than they do their husbands. If moms are not careful, their relationships with their children can begin to supplant the emotionally unsatisfying relationship they have with their husbands.

Some of these mothers also begin to engage their children in a way that is emotionally inappropriate. They begin sharing adult issues with their kids. A woman doesn't feel like she has anyone else to talk to, so she shares her frustration about her husband with her twelve-year-old daughter. How is a twelve-year-old supposed to deal with being brought in to one side of a conflict between her parents? It's impossible. Yet many moms allow their children to become friends and confidants rather than remain children.

One close friend of mine had his wife make an interesting request. "Please don't ever call me 'Momma.'" When asked why, she told him, "I don't want to be just the mother to your children. I am first and foremost your wife." That woman got it right.

A husband expects that his wife will continue to keep him a higher priority than the children. He expects that she will support him and not undermine his authority. He expects that she will save some of her emotional and physical energy for their relationship rather than lavishing it all on her children.

How are you doing in keeping your husband first in your relationship?

These expectations about children and family life are a powerful backdrop to your marriage relationship. Talk about what's going on in your family and how you can have better love now by building a family on biblical principles to the glory of God.

Keeping the Fence Post Solid

Key Concepts about Family Life

- If the rest of your relationships don't work, your marriage won't work.
- Avoid criticizing your spouse's parents.
- Children and grandchildren have the responsibility to take care of aging parents.
- Don't rely on your parents more than you rely on your spouse.
- Involve your parents in appropriate ways, so they can contribute to the process of raising your children.
- A wife wants a husband she can trust with her children.
- A husband wants a mother for his children.
- A husband wants a wife first and a mother second.

Straightening the Post

Discussion for Better Love Now

1. What family relationship causes the most stress in your marriage? Why? What would have to change to make this relationship better?

2. If you could use one word to describe your relationship with your in-laws, what would it be? Why?

3. Are your parents involved in your family life in appropriate ways? Why or why not?

4. Are you fulfilling your role with your children? In what ways is it difficult for you to balance that with your role as a spouse?

Fence Post 5: Respect

"R-E-S-P-E-C-T. Find out what it means to me."

Aretha Franklin's riveting performance of Otis Redding's song came to define the women of a generation. Respect also points to a crucial part of marriage. Without respect, your marriage will soon crumble to dust.

Do you really respect and value your spouse? Do you demonstrate that during conversations and family time or when work needs to be done and decisions need to be made? Those are the moments when a small change in behavior can communicate something essential that leads to better love now.

The next two chapters will help you understand the priority of respect and what it looks like within a marriage. But first, have a short discussion to discover how you both think you're doing now in the area of respect.

Rate your marriage in terms of respect. As with the previous sections, my goal is to get you thinking about each area before you read what I've written and what the Bible says. Have a short, ten-minute discussion with your spouse to prepare you for what God might want to do in your heart.

Fence Post 5: Respect

Wife's Perspective

How would you rate your marriage in the area of respect? Use the following to chart your thoughts.

With a pencil, draw a line on each fence post to show your rating for your marriage in the area of respect.

We honor and value each other.

I wouldn't know respect if I saw it.

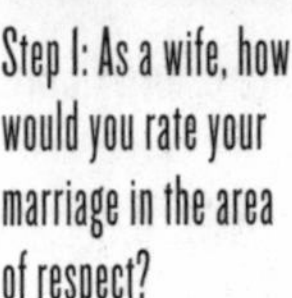

Step 1: As a wife, how would you rate your marriage in the area of respect?

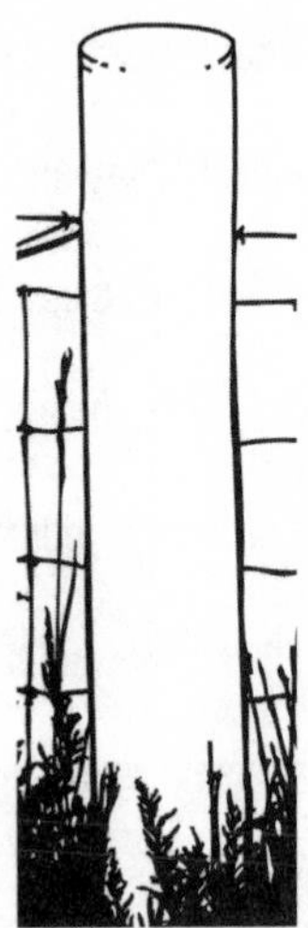

Step 2: How will your husband rate your marriage in the area of respect?

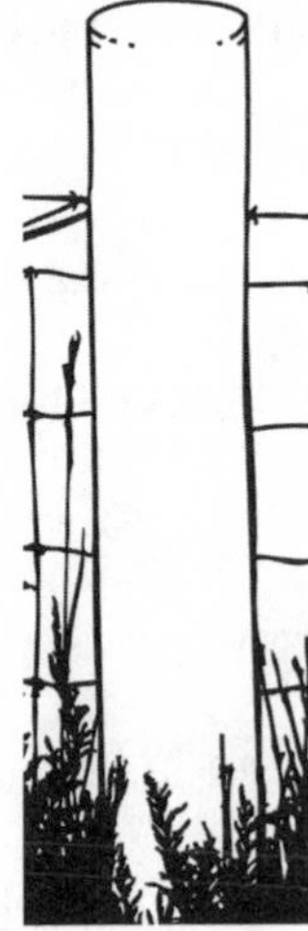

Step 3: What will your husband say you thought? Mark where he will say you rated your marriage in the area of respect.

Fence Post 5: Respect

Husband's Perspective

As a husband, how would you rate your marriage in the area of respect? Use the following to chart your thoughts.

With a pencil, draw a line on each fence post to show your rating in the area of respect.

We honor and value each other.

I wouldn't know respect if I saw it.

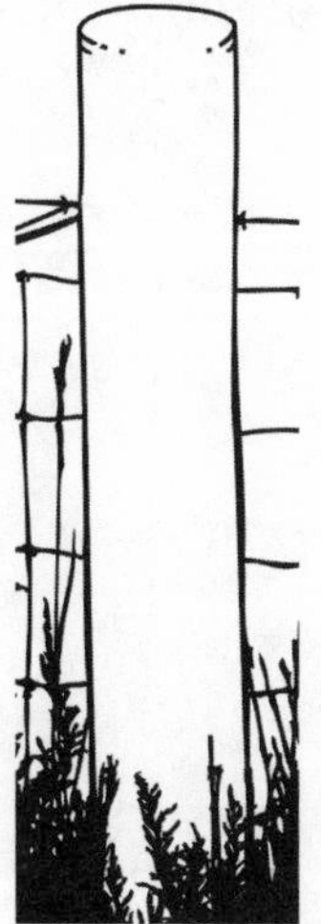

Step 1: As a husband, how would you rate your marriage in the area of respect?

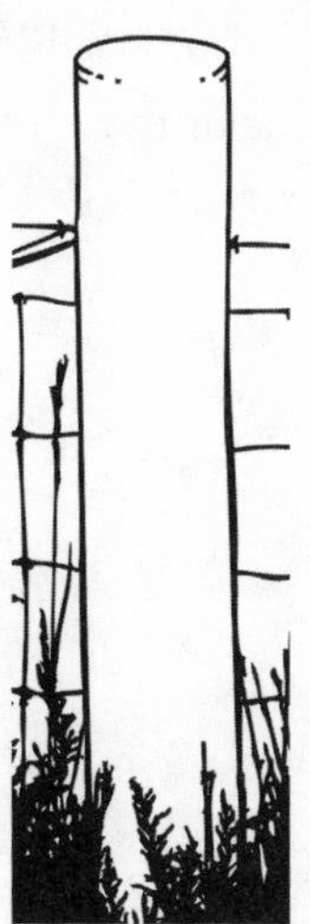

Step 2: How will your wife rate your marriage in the area of respect?

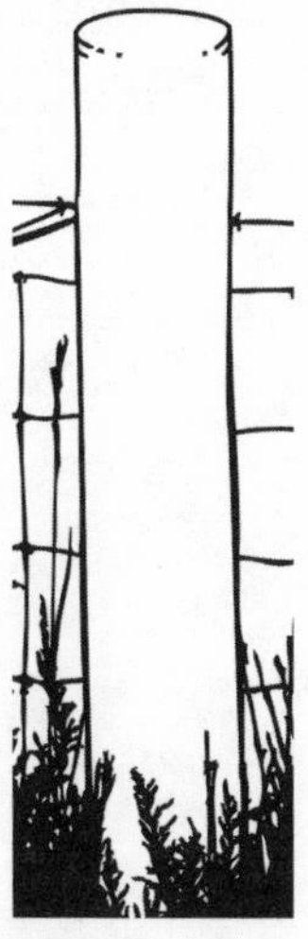

Step 3: What will your wife say you thought? Mark where she will say you rated your marriage in the area of respect.

For Discussion:

You know the drill. Take about ten minutes and work your way from step 1 to step 3. For each step, share why you rated your marriage in the area of respect the way you did. (Note that the wife's step 3 corresponds to the husband's step 2.)

What issues does this raise that you want to consider more deeply? Are there areas in which you and your spouse have a different perspective? Have you seen some potential areas of conflict that need to be addressed?

Have a short prayer, asking God to help you both change in any ways necessary to have better love now.

Now read the chapters and talk through the discussion and application questions at the end.

Chapter 9

Respect and Your Marriage

I CAME ACROSS A STORY recently about a unique "marriage" from another part of the world. After being married to one woman for twenty years, a man decided to take a second wife, something that is allowed in his religion. The story talked about the many consequences of this decision, but perhaps the most interesting one was this: the man admitted that he used the women's jealousy to make them compete to be better wives. He bragged about his ability to get his wives to perform better by manipulating them and their relationship.

What a profound lack of respect. That's a man who is looking at marriage as a way to satisfy his own needs and desires. Self-interest rules his heart and actions, and his wives clearly are not as important or valuable as he thinks he is.

My guess is that there aren't a lot of polygamists reading this book (unless I have a fan base I'm not aware of). But the reality is that all of us struggle with selfishness in our relationships. And marriage is the ultimate petri dish for a selfish heart. Get hitched, drive off in the limo, return from the honeymoon, and watch that selfishness just multiply in your heart. If you let it, it will run rampant and ruin your relationship.

I will never forget the picture-perfect couple whose marriage was a disaster. The wife said in all honesty, "This man, who is supposed to be my head and protector, is my chief adversary. I'm trying to protect myself and my children from their father." Respecting your spouse as one made in the image of God is a critical foundation for having better love now.

The imperative to respect your spouse is fundamental to the Bible. It goes all the way back to the beginning and God's created order. The Bible is clear that man is God's highest creation, his crowning achievement. Because man is made in God's image, every person is worthy of being treated with respect. People have dignity not because of anything they have or haven't done but simply because they are humans. Every single human being is worth more than the whole world put together. This is also why God made Eve from Adam. He could now say, "This one is bone of my bone." So not only did they share dignity because of being made in the image of God, but they also were one flesh. Mutual respect was the first couple's first memory.

When you respect someone, you recognize that they don't just exist for you. Many spouses have become so self-oriented that they consider marriage like a business relationship. They see their spouse as a tool to help them have the kind of life they want to have. Respect means you deem another person as having worth. It also means you then treat them as having worth. This is why James calls loving your neighbor as yourself (James 2:8) the royal law.

When you respect someone, you care more about what they want than what you want. Paul demonstrates this clearly in his letter to the Philippians. They were struggling with their relationships. His solution? "Do nothing from selfishness or empty conceit, but with humility of mind regard one another as more important than yourselves; do not merely look out for your own personal interests, but also for the interests of others. Have this attitude in yourselves which was also in Christ Jesus" (Phil. 2:3–5). Paul goes on to show the depth of Jesus's commitment to meeting our deepest need; he was willing to die on a cross. Respecting your spouse means focusing on "you" before "me." How well are you doing in truly placing your spouse before yourself? That's a diagnostic for respect.

When you respect people, you are attentive to their needs. I did a retreat once with 150 college athletes. I took them to the Last Supper in John and taught on the story of Jesus washing the disciples' feet. Here's Jesus, almighty Lord of the universe, on his hands and knees, doing the work reserved for the lowliest servant. I did my best to preach with power the awesome demonstration of love and respect that Jesus gave on that night.

The room we were in was filled with testosterone. These were macho men. They were the guys who had made it on the fields of battle. They were used to other people washing their clothes, making their dinner, and bringing them towels and water. I looked at those young men and asked them a question. "I want you to fill in the blanks. 'If Jesus can wash the disciple's feet, then I can ________ someone's _________.'" I made every one of those athletes fill in the blanks to find a place of service. I had them make a commitment to serve right there at the retreat. Some said, "I can clean the table for my teammates." Others said, "I can get their food." Or "I can load their cars when they leave."

The retreat was rife with service for the next three days. It was a serving free-for-all. I've never seen anything like it. At the end of the retreat, one of the ladies who worked at the camp said with wonder,

"Who are these young men?" She thought they were part of a holy order. Such is the beauty of respect.

I was trying to reinforce the idea with these young men that every person around them is worthy of respect. It's a dangerous attitude when you start believing your press releases and think you deserve to have people serve you and do nice things for you. It's too easy for all of us to get this way in marriage. When you take your spouse for granted, it will show itself in actions. When you truly respect and cherish your spouse, it will show itself in actions as well.

One of the greatest signs of a lack of respect is a lack of forgiveness. When we hold a grudge or are bitter toward another person, we are in essence saying, "You are not valuable enough for me to care about working this out." When this attitude takes hold in a marriage, it's devastating.

Forgiveness in Marriage

Rheumatoid arthritis is a disease that starts when your immune system turns against your own body and begins to attack it. First the lining of the joints begins to swell. Over time, cells reproduce rapidly, and the lining begins to thicken and get hard. Finally, in the worst stages, the irritated cells release chemicals that damage the bones and tissue around the joints.

One of the cruelest aspects of rheumatoid arthritis is that the very immune system that is supposed to protect your body goes haywire and launches a chain of events that lead to devastation and pain. What was meant to protect you cripples you instead.

This is exactly what happens with an unforgiving spirit in marriage. Husbands and wives are supposed to have the fluid of forgiveness to keep things loose in marriage. But when one person becomes a stickler or judgmental or bitter, then the marriage starts being destroyed from the inside out. An inability to flex and forgive each other causes a marriage to disintegrate.

God wants us to respect each other, so that we will forgive. Marriage is tough enough when you remember how precious your spouse is in the eyes of God. If you begin to forget that on a regular basis, your marriage is in trouble.

It doesn't take very long for me to see that a couple's lack of forgiveness is traumatizing their relationship. Sometimes, there is a serious breach of trust through adultery, misuse of money, abuse, or the like. When a couple like this wants to work it out, I say to the offender, "You *must* change." But to the one whose trust has been violated I say, "You *must* forgive." They cannot *almost* forgive. They cannot hold it in until the next violation and then drag it back out and use it to beat their spouse over the head. I've seen more than one couple say they want to reconcile and then fall apart because they cannot forgive.

Jesus and Forgiveness

Jesus talked a lot about forgiveness. One famous passage occurs in the Gospel of Matthew. "Then Peter came and said to Him, 'Lord, how often shall my brother sin against me and I forgive him? Up to seven times?' Jesus said to him, 'I do not say to you, up to seven times, but up to seventy times seven'" (Matt. 18:21–22).

As is often the case, Peter speaks on behalf of the disciples. He wants to get some clarity on this idea of forgiveness that Jesus has been talking about. So he asks Jesus, "How forgiving do we need to be?" He offers the idea of seven times—a generous number by any measure; many rabbis said three. Imagine someone coming to you seven days in a row to ask forgiveness for the same thing. I'd be pretty sick of seeing them by the fourth or fifth day.

Jesus ups the ante on Peter. He says not seven times, but "seventy times seven"—as many as necessary. Jesus shows Peter that the lifestyle of a Christian must be to forgive.

Jesus goes on to tell the disciples a story.

> *"For this reason the kingdom of heaven may be compared to a king who wished to settle accounts with his slaves. When he had begun to settle them, one who owed him ten thousand talents was brought to him. But since he did not have the means to repay, his lord commanded him to be sold, along with his wife and children and all that he had, and repayment to be made. So the slave fell to the ground and prostrated himself before him, saying, 'Have patience with me and I will repay you everything.' And the lord of that slave felt compassion and released him and forgave him the debt.*
>
> *"But that slave went out and found one of his fellow slaves who owed him a hundred denarii; and he seized him and began to choke him, saying, 'Pay back what you owe.' So his fellow slave fell to the ground and began to plead with him, saying, 'Have patience with me and I will repay you.' But he was unwilling and went and threw him in prison until he should pay back what was owed.*
>
> *"So when his fellow slaves saw what had happened, they were deeply grieved and came and reported to their lord all that had happened. Then summoning him, his lord said to him, 'You wicked slave, I forgave you all that debt because you pleaded with me. Should you not also have had mercy on your fellow slave, in the same way that I had mercy on you?' And his lord, moved with anger, handed him over to the torturers until he should repay all that was owed him."* (Matt. 18:23–34)

In Jesus's story, a king and his accountants go about settling their accounts. One of his subjects owes the king 10,000 talents, or about $35 million. This man is extended grace by the king. It's actually pretty crazy with a debt that size—but the king forgives the man's obligation and tells him he is free to go.

This man then finds another servant who owes him 100 denarii. This was also a significant debt—about 100 days' wages. But instead of offering this man grace like he had received, he deals with him by law and demands his payment.

When the king hears about it, he calls the servant in and deals with him exactly the way he treated his debtor—even using the man's own words against him.

What is the point of this story?

Jesus tells us the point in the Lord's Prayer: "forgive us our debts, as we also have forgiven our debtors" (Matt. 6:12). Paul says it this way: "Whoever has a complaint against anyone; just as the Lord forgave you, so also should you" (Col. 3:13). When we truly experience the forgiveness of God in a way that transforms our hearts, we will want to forgive others.

Why Forgive?

Why should we forgive as Christians? The Bible gives us several reasons:

- We forgive because we are forgiven. Note that God forgives because his wrath was appeased on Calvary. Therefore, with his justice satisfied, God can be merciful to his people.
- God forgives because he is just; we forgive because we are perverse. You and I are both offending criminals against God. What right do we have to stand in judgment of

another criminal and say, "What you have done is so bad that I cannot forgive you"? Whatever offense they have committed against us, it is nothing compared to the offense we have committed against God.

- We forgive because we recognize this other person has equal standing with us before God. We are not on some higher plane of dignity and righteousness. We respect our spouse because they are made in the image of God, and we sympathize because we see reflected in their sin our own fallen status before God.

Respect and forgiveness are vital in marriage because it is an absolute certainty that you are going to hurt your spouse. You can't live in close proximity to another sinful human being and not get hit by the shrapnel of a few relational grenades. It's inevitable.

Think back to the last time your spouse wronged you. How did you handle it? Now think back to the last time you really hurt your spouse. How did they respond? Does the evidence show you respect one another enough to forgive? If you don't, you will have a tough time getting better love now.

What Happens When You Don't Forgive

If you are an unforgiving person, two things begin to happen in your life.

Unforgiving people inevitably become *bitter.* I can honestly say that I have never met a healthy, happy unforgiving person. At first we think it will be fun to play the part of God in judging another person. So we are judgmental and vindictive and harsh. And that can feel good for a few minutes. All that energy and anger rushes out, and our hearts justify our feelings and actions: "My spouse deserves to see and feel how much they have hurt me and how I really feel."

The problem is that God looks good in a royal, purple robe drenched in the blood of his vanquished enemies. When you judge others, you look like a little toddler dressed in adult clothes. It may be cute for a few minutes, but you can't take it seriously.

You and I are not the judge and jury for our spouses. It's not our place to convict them and find them guilty. That's God's job.

If you are holding a grudge against your spouse because they have wronged you, stop right now. If you don't, it will poison your soul. That's why Paul says, "Do not let the sun go down on your anger, and do not give the devil an opportunity" (Eph. 4:26–27). What opportunity? The opportunity to become a bitter and resentful person.

The second thing that happens to unforgiving people is that they become *self-righteous*. The only way you can harbor anger and bitterness is if you think that you aren't that bad. You know, it wasn't that big of a deal for God to pay for your sins and get you into glory. But your spouse? God is going to have to work hard to pull that one off.

It's amazing how subtle the enemy is when he works this into your life. A man settles for a job that his wife thinks is "beneath" him. She wants him to put his resume out and look for a new position, but he never gets around to it. She tries to make peace with it, but the enemy continually reminds her of how much stress his underachieving work places on their finances. She resents him for all the things they can't have and do. Every time a creditor calls, it's like pouring salt in the open wound.

And she begins to think about how much more diligent and responsible she is. Over the years, she loses respect for him and certainly won't forgive him. She becomes a bitter and self-righteous person.

I've seen this with husbands and wives—they drive a wedge through their marriage. What about your marriage? Are you harboring unforgiveness in your heart?

How Can You Forgive?

In Luke 17, Jesus tells an unusual parable about forgiveness:

"Be on your guard! If your brother sins, rebuke him; and if he repents, forgive him. And if he sins against you seven times a day, and returns to you seven times, saying, 'I repent,' forgive him." And the apostles said to the Lord, "Increase our faith!" The Lord said, "If you had faith like a mustard seed, you would say to this mulberry tree, 'Be uprooted and be planted in the sea'; and it would obey you.

"Which of you, having a slave plowing or tending sheep, will say to him when he has come in from the field, 'Come immediately and sit down to eat'? But will he not say to him, 'Prepare something for me to eat, and properly clothe yourself and serve me while I eat and drink; and afterward you may eat and drink'? He does not thank the slave because he did the things which were commanded, does he?

"So you too, when you do all the things which are commanded you, say, 'We are unworthy slaves; we have done only that which we ought to have done.'" (Luke 17:3–10)

In verse 3, Jesus is explicitly warning his disciples against bitterness and self-righteousness. He commands them to forgive—even seven times a day, if necessary.

The disciples heard what Jesus said and had the same reaction you and I would. How do you feel when someone really does you wrong? When you find out someone at church has been talking about you behind your back? When you discover that league politics means your child won't be on the all-star team? When a classmate has spread a vicious rumor about your daughter? When you realize that your co-worker is taking credit for the big project you helped finish?

Some of the people reading this book have been deeply wronged. Maybe you were sexually abused as a child. Maybe you were worked over by a father or a mother. Maybe you were swindled out of your nest egg by a greedy partner. Perhaps a drunk driver took the life of someone you love.

I know I wouldn't feel like forgiving in those situations. And I certainly wouldn't feel like forgiving people like that seven times in a day. The disciples had the same reaction. They said, "If this is what we have to do, then we are going to need more faith."

Here's the crazy, almost unspiritual thing about this passage. Jesus says it doesn't take great faith to forgive. He tells the disciples in verse 6 that if they have faith as small as a mustard seed, they can do much more miraculous things than forgive. So what do you need if you don't need more faith?

Jesus asks the disciples to put themselves in his place. Imagine that you are the master. Would you want your servants doing what they felt like doing or what you told them to do?

He says to them, and I paraphrase, "If you had a servant working in a field, when he came in would you tell him to sit down and eat right away? Or would you tell him to fix your dinner and serve you and then get himself something to eat?"

A servant who has been working in the field all day is going to come in tired and hungry. You can imagine him working in the kitchen, preparing some creamy mashed potatoes, some good country gravy, maybe a nice medium sirloin, and a big salad with some ranch dressing. Boy, it sure looks good.

That servant doesn't want to serve that food to his master; he wants to sit down and eat it himself. But he doesn't. He serves his master first before taking care of himself. And the master doesn't even have to thank the servant because the servant is just doing what he is paid to do.

Jesus says the same thing should be true of us when it comes to forgiveness. He says, "You don't need feelings and faith; you just need to do what I told you to do."

I hate that passage. I think it's unspiritual. But God knows I need this parable. It runs counter to all of my emotions. When people really do me wrong, I want to speak to them with some words I couldn't put in this book. I want to stomp 'em. I want to make a few phone calls to share a "prayer request." I want others to join in my bitterness and sense of injustice.

I do not feel like greeting them, praying for them, speaking well of them, much less giving them food and drink and blessing them.

And it's even worse when it's my wife.

But Jesus says, "I don't expect you to feel a certain way; I just expect you to obey me."

You don't have to feel like forgiving, but you do have to forgive. You do have to be quiet and not slander. You have to be kind. You have to respond according to the divine standard that God has given.

I know it's a lot easier to write and read about forgiveness than it is to actually forgive. But it's the command of the King. If you are harboring unforgiveness and disrespect in your heart toward your spouse, you are absolutely disobeying Jesus Christ. You need to repent and do what Jesus has told you to do.

Do it for yourself, for your spouse, and for the glory of God. Marriage makes disrespect show up like a velvet Elvis poster under a black light. If you disrespect your spouse, they will know it and will have to live with the consequences every day. You'll keep getting more and more bitter, and you won't have the joy of living in obedience.

God has more for you than that. Find it by letting go, respecting your spouse before God, and forgiving them in Christ. Cultivating respect for your spouse keeps the fence post solid and enables you to have better love now. How do you need to forgive?

Chapter 10

What Your Spouse Expects Concerning Respect

I JUST SPENT A CHAPTER convincing you that to have better love now, you must make sure that an atmosphere of respect pervades your marriage and your home. The Bible commands it, the created order supports it, and our marriages depend on it.

But how does a woman experience respect?

A Wife Expects Honor

When your wife heard you say, "I do," at the altar, she expected you would honor her. She believed you would treat her well.

First Peter 3:7 could not be any clearer on this point. It tells men we should grant our wives honor "as a fellow heir of the grace of life." The "grace of life" is the salvation that is in Jesus Christ. Your wife is a sister to you in grace; she is your equal before God.

The Bible clearly teaches the authority of a husband in the home. It also clearly teaches that men are to lead as elders, deacons, and pastors. But it just as clearly teaches that in the grace of life, women and men are equals.

This is one area where men don't have a very good track record.

That's why in the Song of Solomon, before they are married, the man says to the woman,

"O my dove, in the clefts of the rock,
In the secret place of the steep pathway,
Let me see your form,
Let me hear your voice;
For your voice is sweet,
And your form is lovely." (Song of Sol. 2:14)

The thought being, I'm not going to hurt you. Historically, women have been abused by men, raped by men, murdered by men, and bought and sold by men. This man says, "Little dove, come out, I'm not going to hurt you." Godly men understand that in Christ both man and woman are redeemed to be who God intended them to be.

Have you ever noticed how often you see women in the Bible? This is quite different from other ancient literature. In most writing from the ancient world, women played a very small role. They were treated as property, as inferiors, or as insignificant.

But that's not the way it is in the Bible. At the cross, there are women. At the tomb, more women. There are women who financially supported Jesus. There are women who are the focus of his time and attention. There are women who experienced his healing and forgiveness.

The New Testament elevates women because Christ restores the glory of who a woman really is before God. A woman is to be honored as a fellow heir in the grace of life.

Proverbs 31 says to a man, "Give her the product of her hands" (v. 31). Her husband praises her in the gates, and says, "Many daughters have done nobly, but you excel them all" (v. 29). "Give her the product of her hands" means she needs a payday. A woman should be compensated for her work as a wife and a mother. And part of that compensation is that the man sits in the gates of the city and says to all who pass by, "Many daughters have done nobly, but I want to show you a picture of my wife." A man, in the way he speaks to a woman and about a woman, can honor her.

We spend our lives looking for people who respect us, like us, and honor us because we can't produce that effect for ourselves. James Dobson says single people produce a hormone that declines significantly once they get married—it's a desire to give someone honor and esteem. When you started dating, you naturally honored and esteemed your date. A man pulls out her chair, he helps her sit down, he listens to her when she talks, he pats her on the hand. She laughs at his jokes, admires his accomplishments ("You scored how many touchdowns? You are a strong man"). They supply the "honor hormone" to each other.

But things change after marriage, especially for men. Once a man gets married, he says, "Well, I accomplished it." Men go after wives like hunters go after an elk. He sees the one he likes, gets her in his sights, brings her down, and puts her on the wall. "Not bad, not bad. Is dinner ready?" Men tend to slip into neutral, treating their wives as another tool to help them have the life they want.

So a man dates a woman for a year or two and supplies heavy doses of esteem and honor all during that time. The glands are secreting honor hormone all over the place. Now, after two or three years of a bone-dry marriage, what's going to happen? The woman longs for the honor that her husband used to give her, and she'll eventually find it somewhere.

She may invest herself in all kinds of things to try to find that honor. She'll have the nicest home, the best kids, be the ultimate volunteer, have a dynamic career. All women will do something to find the esteem they're not receiving from their husband. All people need that hormone. She's looking for something or someone who can supply it. And so, husbands, even though it's not an instinct anymore, you must make it a discipline. No matter what else is going on, you just need to stop at some point every day, suck it up, and say, "Whew, all right, it's on. Here we go." Then you need to honor your wife.

When they don't receive honor from their husbands, many women turn to other things to build their lives around. Have you ever seen a woman who doesn't really have a marriage anymore, just her relationship with the kids? She is seeking from her children what her husband is not providing.

Or you've met women who are committed to their careers at the expense of their families. Often this is a long process that grows out of finding a level of honor and respect in the workplace that they don't get at home. Her work is no longer a means to do what she enjoys doing. Instead, on her hiring anniversary, there is a man there with flowers who tells her how much he appreciates all that she does. She has co-workers who congratulate her at the end of the big project or the conclusion of the big sale.

Women will find something somewhere to give them a sense of esteem. So imagine a woman who doesn't receive honor at home. She goes to work one Tuesday and then heads out to lunch with the gang at Chili's. There's a guy there in the next booth, and their eyes meet, and he smiles. His eyes linger for a moment. She hasn't had a guy look at her that way in eighteen months. After he pays his check, he stops by the table. "Do you come here often?" he asks. "Where do you all work?" "Do you really? Wow, I've heard great things about that place. You must be really sharp. I know how they hire only the best. So, do you have a doctorate?"

You can imagine how she feels; it's just pumping her up. "Do you come here every Tuesday?" What's she going to say? And that next Tuesday, how does she dress to go to work? I'm just a mortal man, but I can figure out how to break a marriage up when there is no esteem. What if you're Satan? I'll guarantee you he'll get right in there and make a mess. He's doing it all the time.

Men, if you wake up to a strange concoction on a plate, don't say, "Is that breakfast or a burnt offering?" You look her straight in the eye and say, "Honey, looks good to me!" Find ways every day to honor your wife.

A woman needs to feel honored with her children. This is vitally important. Honor your wife to your children. I've told my sons, "Marry a woman like your momma and you'll do fine." I've always extolled my wife to my children. I'm glad that I did that.

This is important because kids always challenge their mother's authority. They will bow up on Momma about what to eat, what to wear, and who to run around with. A good father knows to nip that stuff in the bud. As soon as they cross that line, you just say, "It's time to head for the woodshed." I let my sons know you don't cross this line with this woman. "This woman right here spent about eighteen hours in labor with you. You live because of her. Every part of your body was on loan from her. She was in labor while I was reading *Field and Stream*. If you cross the line with her, me and you are going to get it on." Your wife needs to know that you have her back when it comes to the children. That's one of the ways she feels honored.

John Walvoord is one of my heroes. He was one of the greatest theological thinkers in the history of our country. The last time he spoke in a chapel at Dallas Seminary before his death, there were 500 men in complete silence listening to this ninety-year-old systematic theologian speak. What do you think he chose to speak about for his last chapel message? He spoke about honoring your wives.

He was so old that he had to get a stool because his knees wouldn't hold him up anymore. He said, "You know, guys," as he leaned against the podium, "in my day we didn't put our arms around our wives and hug them and kiss them. I don't know why, but in my day, in the early 1900s, we just didn't. And my father, who was born in about 1860, he didn't either. But you know what I've learned in my later days? Every day I say to my wife, 'I love you, I cherish you, and I honor you.'"

The chaplain of the seminary left the chapel after the message and went to the parking lot. His son was a student at the seminary, and he saw him standing by his car, drying his eyes with a tissue.

He asked, "What's the matter, son?"

His son replied, "Dr. Walvoord really nailed me. To see a ninety-year-old man tell us, 'You know, I didn't always do it right, but I am trying to now.' I want to be a man like that."

That's the message for a husband to a wife. "I may not have always done it right. I'm trying to now. I love you. I honor you. And I will cherish you today and every day."

A Wife Expects Appreciation

Another key thing a woman expected when she heard her husband say, "I do," was that he would appreciate her and show it.

Mother's Day needs to happen a lot more than just once a year. Husbands need to consistently and continually appreciate their wives.

It can be difficult for women in our culture to feel appreciated. What do we appreciate and celebrate about women today? When you pass by the magazine stands, do you see *Godly Housewife Illustrated?* No, it's all about bodies and beauty. Who's going to praise a woman who is consistently running her household well? Is the media going to praise her? Is Hollywood going to praise her? Are magazines going to praise her? Are authors going to praise her? Nobody's going to praise her but her husband. If he doesn't do it, no one will.

Here's an exercise: walk up to your wife, put your hands on her shoulders, and look into her eyes. Then, for the next thirty seconds, without looking away, tell her how much she means to you and how you appreciate all she does. Even with her fallibilities and failures, thank her for being a good in-law to your parents, a mother to your children, a friend to your friends, and for taking care of your home. You'll probably get choked up and start squeaking about halfway through. And if you do make it for thirty seconds, you better have a strong grip on those shoulders because your wife might faint.

When I do weddings, the same thing always happens: after the couple turns to face each other to say their vows, the groom invariably turns and starts saying his vows to me, "Sally, I love you." Why do they do that? Because when a man looks at his beautiful bride, he chokes up. My son, the tough guy, choked up and couldn't say a word at his wedding. That's the way we men are.

We need to bring that same sense of appreciation into our marriage. Husbands, tell your wife what you think about her, that she's precious to you.

Peter Marshall was a great Presbyterian minister. He preached a famous message that began with the story of a city that had a beautiful mountain pool in the center of town. The people hired a man to be the keeper of the spring. His job was to make sure the spring and streams that fed the water of the city were always clean and pure. He roamed the hillsides around town, removing any debris or trash that could contaminate the waters.

The town's pool was extraordinary. The mountains and clouds reflected off its crystal surface. The water was clear and pure and sought after by people from all around the area. The city began to grow, in part because of the beauty of this little lake.

As the size of the city increased, they incurred lots of additional expenses. At one town meeting, they noticed the budget item for the keeper of the spring. They didn't see much of the old man in town. They figured it couldn't be that hard to keep the streams clean. For all they knew, he was just off in the hills somewhere, and the waters pretty much took care of themselves. So they fired the keeper of the spring.

It wasn't long before the water in the pool had a brownish hue. It began to smell. Slime and algae began to grow on the rocks on the sides of the lake. People in the city became sick. The spring had become contaminated and was no longer good for drinking. The pool was no longer a showplace in the center of the community. They discovered that the job they thought was disposable was the only thing that allowed the city to be a showpiece.

Do you know what Sunday of the year Peter Marshall preached his sermon called "The Keeper of the Spring"? It was Mother's Day. That's what a mother is in our culture. She is the keeper of the spring. And we look past her and take her for granted. Then, when she is no longer there, our families suffer incredible devastation. Appreciate your wife—she deserves it.

A Husband Expects Respect

For a man, when he heard his wife say, "I do," at the altar, he was expecting to receive respect.

This is the most important thing a man wants from his wife—do this and almost all the other needs take care of themselves. He wants to be respected. "The wife must see to it that she respects her husband" (Eph. 5:33b). The book of Proverbs says, "The heart of her husband trusts in her, . . . She does him good and not evil / All the days of her life" (31:11a, 12). (And every husband's favorite verse: "Sarah obeyed Abraham, calling him lord" [1 Pet. 3:6].)

Remember the "honor hormone" we discussed? Men need it too. Men spend their entire lives looking for respect. Women are great at giving this to men when they are dating in the way they speak to men, the way they speak about men, the way they treat men, the way they listen to men—it all communicates an attitude of respect. That's a powerful draw to a man.

After women marry their men, showing respect to their husband has to move from an instinct to a discipline.

When a man doesn't feel respected at home, he gets strange and crazy. He'll start looking to something outside the home he hopes will make him feel good about himself.

Men turn into idiots when they don't get respect. They do incredibly stupid things: materialism, workaholism, pornography, adultery. When a man feels that his wife doesn't care for him, respect him, or value him, it's much more difficult for him to resist temptation.

One important aspect of respect is how you treat your husband in the privacy of your home. How do you speak to your husband, especially in front of your children? Have you had to apologize to your children for how you treated your husband? On rare occasions my wife had to do that. She went to my two sons and said, "I need to ask your forgiveness because of the way I spoke to your father." One son would always say, "No problem." My smart-aleck son would say, "I'm going to start doing drugs now. I'm quitting school. My life is going down the tubes."

Privately treat your husband with honor, respect, and dignity. Do not talk to him like he is stupid or the enemy. Even when you are frustrated, remember you are on the same team. Talk to him with a tone of voice that lets him and others know that you respect him as the spiritual leader of your home.

Respect also determines how you treat your husband publicly. Have you ever seen a man disrespected by his wife in public? That is a sad and awkward situation. I remember a dinner party we attended with about six couples. It was a beautiful home and a wonderful dinner. The husband was helping his wife, and he made the mistake of bringing in one of the dishes too early. His wife, out of nowhere, reproves him in the harshest way. "Would you get that out of here? When I want that in here, I'll tell you!" You could see him shrink and shrivel with humiliation. I was thinking, *Boy, if she does this publicly, what is she like in private?* (He died a few years later, and I couldn't help but have the fleeting thought that God had at least delivered him from her disrespect.)

Respect is also shown in the way a wife obeys and follows her husband. If a wife respects her husband, then after the praying and the dialogue, she trusts him and says, "I'll go with you on this. I'll follow you."

Can you imagine what it must have been like to be Mary? God appeared to Joseph in a dream, "You need to marry Mary." God appeared to Joseph in another dream, "You need to leave Bethlehem and travel to Egypt." God appeared again to Joseph in a dream, "Those who sought the child's life are dead, you need to go back home." So they travel back. Mary says, "Are we going to Bethlehem?" Joseph has another dream. "No, we're going back to Nazareth." Mary could easily have gotten tired of following him. After all, Joseph was having the dreams, not her. She could have said, "Dream or no dream, we aren't leaving until God tells me."

There had to be times when it was difficult for Priscilla to follow Aquila. Can you imagine the conversation in their house? "You know that guy who everyone wants to kill or throw out of town? Why don't we ask him to move in with us? Paul can teach when the church meets in our house." Meanwhile, 20,000 people gathered at an amphitheater and called for the death of Paul. So Priscilla was a woman of great faith who had respect for her husband.

A wife has every right to confer with her husband and let her two cents be known. But, as in any relationship, sometimes your six or eight cents can't be known. Respect means that you say, "I'm going to trust you."

My wife has said to me, "Look, I don't agree completely with what you're thinking, but I'm going to trust you because you are the one who will have to give account to the Almighty." Thanks for the reminder.

So respect doesn't mean that you always agree with your husband. Men, when your wife has a problem with something you are doing, you need to listen hard. She could be God's voice to keep you from evil.

Does respect mean a wife always obeys her husband? Sometimes a wife has to make a difficult choice. Consider Sapphira in the book of Acts. Her husband sold a piece of real estate, gave some of the proceeds to the apostles, but held back part of it for himself, then lied and said he gave everything. What happened to Ananias? He dropped dead.

Sapphira came in and Peter said, "Did you sell this land for $5,000?"

"Yes, we did." She carried out her husband's lie. And she dropped dead too. She was judged because she submitted to her husband in an evil action. A woman should not submit to something criminal, evil, or immoral.

Have you read the story of Abigail in the Bible? She is the patron saint of rebellious women. All women love Abigail once they hear the story (1 Sam. 25). Her husband was named *Nabal* (which means "fool"). Here's a little extra piece of free advice—be careful about marrying a guy named Nabal. The next time you meet a guy named Idiot Johnson, or something like that, it'd probably be a good idea to think twice about marrying him.

Nabal had flocks of animals traveling in the wilderness with shepherds who tended them. David had protected Nabal's shepherds from their enemies, so David sent some servants to see about getting food from Nabal's slaughter and harvest. Nabal sent them back empty-handed, greatly offending David.

When Abigail heard about the stupid thing Nabal had done, she intervened and sent donkeys with food and gifts ahead to David before he could bring judgment on Nabal. David received the gifts and relented.

There are times when a woman has to obey God rather than her husband. You'll know it when it happens. That's all part of obedience. By and large, you'll show respect to your husband by how you treat him in private and public. And in the final analysis you need to say, like Mary and Priscilla, "I'm going to trust you; I'm going to go with you."

The primary need a man has is the respect of his wife.

A Husband Expects an Attractive Wife

What else does a man expect when he hears his wife say, "I do"? Some of you may think this one doesn't belong in this book, but I can assure you it does. A man expects to have *a wife who is attractive.* Let me explain what I mean. I've never met a man who married a woman as an act of mercy. A man doesn't look at a woman and say, "Yes, God, who else will take this poor creature?" No man is attracted to a woman because she's ugly. And that's OK.

The Bible says about the woman in Proverbs 31:22, "She makes coverings for herself. Her clothing is fine linen and purple." She took care of herself.

A woman in our church is a missionary in China with her husband. A few years ago they came over for lunch. I had seen her every few years, and each time I saw her, she had thicker and thicker glasses. That day at lunch I was looking at her and knew something had changed. She had always been attractive, but something was different. I finally realized she didn't have glasses on. So I said, "What happened to your glasses?" I loved her answer. I'm not saying it's right for every woman.

She said, "I was looking at myself day after day with those Coke-bottle glasses, and one day I thought, 'My husband didn't marry the woman I see in the mirror. I'm going to do something about it.'" She had corrective surgery done on her eyes, so she no longer needed glasses.

Of course there is nothing wrong with wearing glasses. It's her attitude that was interesting to me. She said, "I'm going to do what I've got to do to be pretty for my husband." She wanted to stay attractive in her marriage. She respected her husband enough to care.

Everyone who is married knows that marriage changes your appearance. As we get older, we thicken like a ballpark frank. When I look at my wedding picture, I know my wife can't get into her wedding gown and I can't get into that $38 tux. But even though we can't fit into the clothes, I want at least the picture of us to be able to fit into the frame. It takes work to stay attractive in marriage. It takes discipline about eating and exercise, but it is a spiritual effort that we do for our mate.

A Husband Expects Appreciation

When a man hears his wife say, "I do," at the altar, he expects she will appreciate him. If you want better love now, learn to tangibly demonstrate your appreciation to your husband.

For men who go out into the rat race, they find that, by and large, the rats are winning. A lot of men go out there and just get lathered up for about forty years and then die in the harness. And during that time, they would like to know that their efforts are appreciated.

I talked to a guy recently whose marriage was coming apart. I asked him what he thought the basic problem was. After a few questions and short answers, he finally got to the meat of the issue: "I feel like a pack mule. I do my best. I go out and work and provide everything that I can provide. Everybody takes, but nobody really cares. It's just like at work. I own a restaurant. I hire people who aren't exactly aspiring to be career busboys. I try to keep them in line but end up firing about one every month for employee theft. Everybody lives off my hard work, but nobody really cares what I go through."

As he was talking, I watched a hard-charging businessman become a little kid crying on the side of a playground: "Nobody cares what I go through." He went on to say, "I would at least like somebody to say, 'Thanks for going down in that pit and doing what you've got to do.'" That's a valid consideration, and every man feels the same way.

One of the best movie scenes ever is from *The African Queen* with Humphrey Bogart and Katharine Hepburn. Do you remember the scene where they are in the marsh and the boat won't move anymore? Humphrey Bogart climbs out of the boat, grabs a rope, and starts pulling the boat through the swamp. He pulls and pulls until he's completely exhausted. He climbs up into the boat and takes off his shirt. Katharine Hepburn reels back in horror. What does she see all over Humphrey Bogart? Leeches. You can see him shiver on the screen (what an actor!). "Ohhhh, I hate these little buggers!" One by one they get the leeches off him. He's shivering because he hates having leeches on him. Then they sit there in a pregnant silence.

Katharine Hepburn and Humphrey Bogart just look at each other because the fact is, the boat isn't moving on its own. And even though they don't say a word, everybody's thinking the same thing. He looks at her and, without saying a word, puts on his shirt and climbs out of the boat. You can see Katharine Hepburn's heart break as she looks at him. Ultimately, she climbs out of the boat and gets down there with him. That's sometimes how a man feels about going to work—"I've got to get down there with those little leeches." So a man just wants to know he is appreciated. Most men don't mind giving their lives down there as long as somebody says, "Good job. Good job."

A Husband Expects a Wife Who Is His Crown

When a man hears his wife say, "I do," at the altar, he believes he is going to get a wife who will be a crown to him. Proverbs 12:4 says, "An excellent wife is the crown of her husband, but she who shames him is like rottenness in his bones." The deepest pain a man has is a wife who is not respected by other people. Sometimes when I get down, I encourage myself by saying, "Well, you know, Teresa married me; I must be a pretty good guy." In all of my years of being married—I thank God for this—she has never shamed me. Everybody respects her. Everybody likes her because she is kind, loving, and giving. She's a good daughter-in-law to my parents; she is a good mother to my children; she is now a good grandmother to my grandchildren. The women of our church respect her.

The highest compliment a man can give another man is to compliment his wife. I walk up to Harry and say, "Harry, how did some old, broken down, sorry guy like yourself ever get Harriet to marry you?" How do you think Harry will respond to that question? Normally he'd be offended (about the "broken down, sorry" part). But in this case he'll puff up his chest a little bit and say, "Actually, I'm sorrier than you know." The highest compliment you can give a man is to insult him by asking how someone as great as his wife would have ever married him. When you esteem a man's wife, you esteem the man. Whenever you glorify a man's wife, you glorify the man. (As an aside, just a little bit of expert advice—I wouldn't suggest trying this with women: "How did an ugly thing like yourself hook up with a stud like your husband?")

I'm not sure how I would handle it if I were married to a woman that nobody liked. You've probably met some couples where a guy was married to a woman who made you wonder if he had done something horrible in a previous life. She can't get along with anyone; it's almost painful to watch. That's a very difficult situation for a man to handle.

Proverbs 11:22 says, "As a ring of gold in a swine's snout, so is a beautiful woman who lacks discretion." If you saw a pig with a gold ring in its nose, would you stop and say, "You know, that's not a bad-looking pig?" Does the ring cancel out the ugliness? It doesn't. Instead you'd be thinking, *What a waste of jewelry to put a gold ring on this pig.* When you see a great-looking woman who has no character, her looks are canceled out by her lack of character.

If you remember *Little House on the Prairie*, you also probably remember the Ingalls' neighbor, Nels Olsen. Didn't you just hurt for that guy? Every time I watched one of those episodes, I would cringe when his wife, Harriet, came on the screen. Nels spent all of his time trying to excuse Harriet's behavior. It seemed his favorite words were "Harriet means well."

No man likes to be forced to explain his wife's actions or attitude to people: "Forgive her; she woke up on the bad side of the broom this morning." Men are tortured by that experience, even if they don't show it on the outside. Every man wants a wife who is an honor to him, whom he can brag about, who is a crown for his head.

How are you doing in helping your spouse respect you? How are you doing in respecting and honoring your spouse? Meet these expectations as you live with each other, and you'll generate powerful momentum to help you have better love now.

Keeping the Fence Post Solid

Key Concepts about Respect

- Marriage is the ultimate petri dish for a selfish heart.
- When you respect someone, you care more about what they want than what you want.
- I have never met a healthy, happy, unforgiving person.
- You don't have to feel like forgiving, but you do have to forgive.
- To respect your wife, you must honor her.
- Show your wife respect by giving her appreciation.
- Men spend their entire lives looking for respect.
- Show your husband respect by being an attractive wife.
- Show your husband respect by giving him appreciation.
- Show your husband respect by being a wife who is a crown.

Straightening the Post

Discussion for Better Love Now

1. Why do you think respect is so important in marriage? How do you feel when you see couples show a lack of respect?

2. What makes it hard for us to forgive others? What have you had to forgive in your marriage? How well have you done?

3. How well do you do at showing honor and appreciation to your spouse? What works to help your spouse feel respected?

4. As a husband, how are you doing about meeting your wife's expectations for respect? What do you need to work on the most?

5. As a wife, how are you doing in meeting your husband's expectations for respect? What do you need to work on the most?

Fence Post 6: Sex

You can't write a book on marriage without talking about sex. Often the things that are most central to our humanity are the things Satan distorts in the cruelest ways. That's certainly true of sex.

Sex is the physical expression of your one-flesh union with your spouse. It's very important and one of the most prominent areas of stress and disagreement in marriage.

Trying to ignore it doesn't make any sense. Our culture is saturated with it. People talk about it. Men and women want it. You may as well be honest and willing to learn and grow based on God's Word and the desires of your spouse.

The next two chapters will help you understand the role of sex in marriage. But first, have a short discussion to discover how you both think you're doing now with your sexuality.

Rate your marriage in terms of sex. As with the previous sections, my goal is to get you thinking about each area before you read what I've written and what the Bible says. I'm again hoping you'll have a short, ten-minute discussion with your spouse to prepare you for what God might want to do in your heart.

Fence Post 6: Sex

Wife's Perspective

How would you rate the sexual aspect of your marriage? Use the following to chart your thoughts.

With a pencil, draw a line on each fence post to show your rating for your marriage in the area of sex.

We have sex the right amount and in the right way—it's awesome!

Our sexual relationship is dissatisfying.

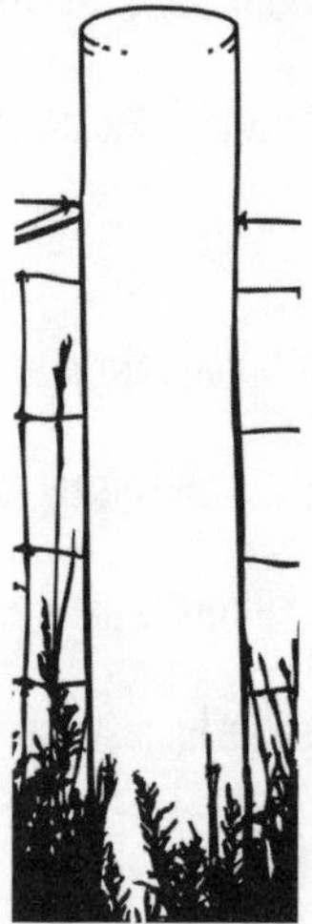

Step 1: As a wife, how would you rate the sex in your marriage?

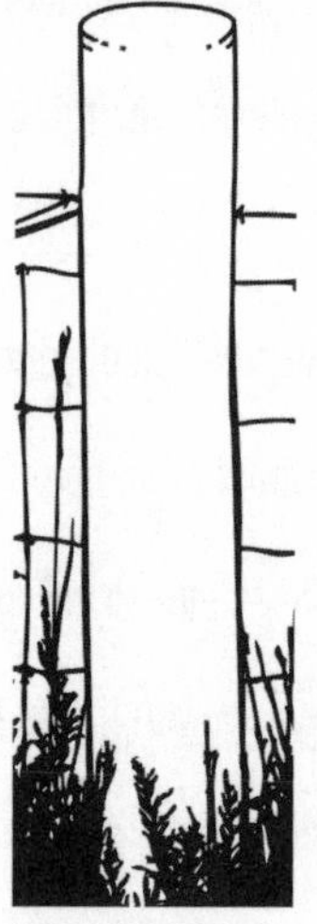

Step 2: How will your husband rate the sex in your marriage?

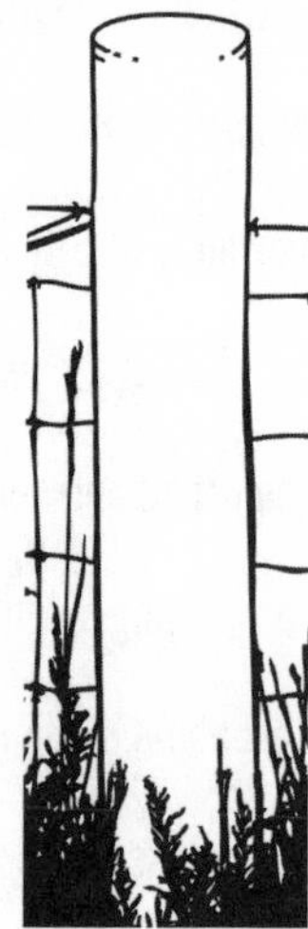

Step 3: What will your husband say you thought? Mark where he will say you rated the sex in your marriage.

Fence Post 6: Sex

Husband's Perspective

As a husband, how would you rate your marriage in terms of sex? Use the following to chart your thoughts.

With a pencil, draw a line on each fence post to show your rating in the area of sex.

We have sex the right amount and in the right way—it's awesome!

Our sexual relationship is dissatisfying.

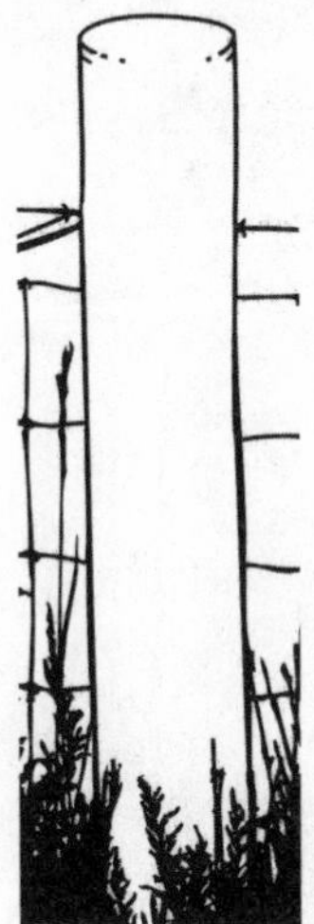

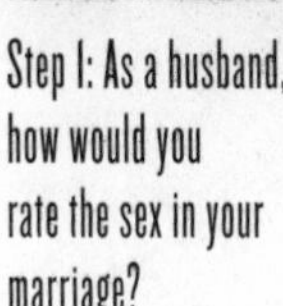

Step 1: As a husband, how would you rate the sex in your marriage?

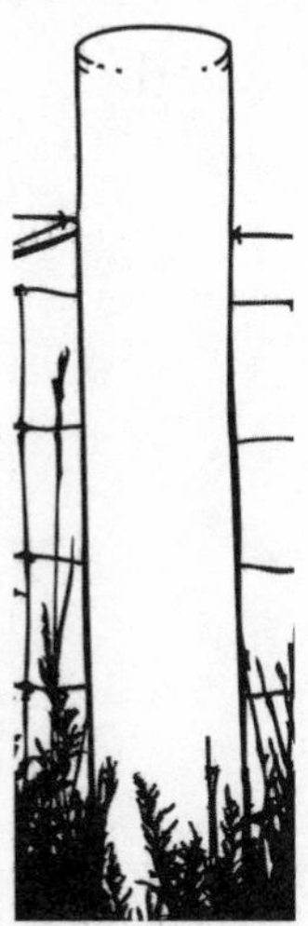

Step 2: How will your wife rate the sex in your marriage?

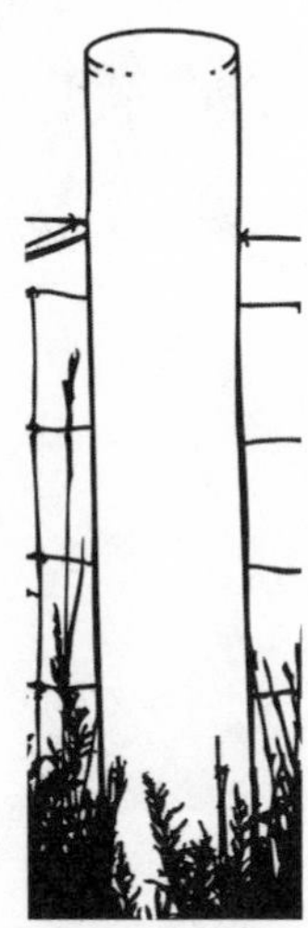

Step 3: What will your wife say you thought? Mark where she will say you rated the sex in your marriage.

For Discussion:

You know the drill. Take about ten minutes and work your way from step 1 to step 3. For each step, share why you rated your sexual relationship the way you did. (Note that the wife's step 3 corresponds to the husband's step 2.)

What issues does this raise that you want to consider more deeply? Are there areas in which you and your spouse have a different perspective? Have you seen some potential areas of conflict that need to be addressed?

Have a short prayer, asking God to help you both change in any ways necessary to have better love now.

Now read the chapters and talk through the discussion and application questions at the end.

Chapter 11

Intimacy and Sex in Marriage

IMAGINE THAT YOU AND I take a boat trip together down a river in the jungle. Our guide brings us to a small village at a bend in the river. While we sit around sharing a meal with the locals, a large crocodile appears, grabs a young man at the edge of the village, and disappears back to the river.

We are shocked, to say the least. But we are even more shocked by the reaction of the other villagers—they don't react at all. Even as the crocodile splashes back into the river, the men and women of the village continue the meal with apparent indifference.

Then you notice something interesting about the villagers. A man on your left is missing a leg. A woman on your right is missing an arm. A young man lying down in the circle appears to have lost both legs.

Finally, curiosity gets the best of us and we discreetly ask our guide what is going on. He tells us that the crocodiles of the river eat the villagers on a regular basis, but they never acknowledge the crocodiles. They never even talk about them.

You ask the guide, "Why don't they set traps for the crocodiles or place watchmen outside the village to warn when the crocodiles approach?"

"They could do that, but they don't want to scare or offend any of the other villagers. They've decided they would prefer to act as if the crocodiles don't exist."

This parable portrays the church's behavior when it comes to sex in our culture today. Men and women are being maimed left and right by inappropriate sex, and most of our church leaders are afraid to talk about it because they might offend someone's sensibilities.

I crossed that bridge a long time ago. I decided it was way too important to be afraid to talk frankly about sex. In my Song of Solomon conferences and in *The Book of Romance*, we deal in detail about the sexual relationship of a man and woman.

You won't have better love now unless you have good sex. It's too central to what marriage is all about. In this chapter, I'm going to give you a little of the biblical basis of sexuality, then warn you of the dangers sex can bring to a marriage. The next chapter will deal with some of the expectations of both men and women regarding sex.

In 1 Corinthians 7:2–5, Paul makes it clear that sex is a good thing and a gift from God: "But because of immoralities, each man is to have his own wife, and each woman is to have her own husband. The husband must fulfill his duty to his wife, and likewise also the wife to her husband. The wife does not have authority over her own body, but the husband does; and likewise also the husband does not have authority over his own body, but the wife does. Stop depriving one another, except by agreement for a time, so that you may devote yourselves to prayer, and come together again so that Satan will not tempt you because of your lack of self-control."

From the beginning, when God declared that men and women were to be "one flesh," it is clear that sex is a wonderful part of God's plan for marriage. A proper meeting of the sex drive is a valid need and expectation in marriage. Paul even says that you have an obligation to meet the sexual needs of your spouse, to give yourself to each other. Your body is no longer your own to command; you now have to consider your spouse's needs and desires as more important than your own.

First Corinthians 7:5 is the one verse in the Bible that describes frigidity. Paul says to "stop depriving one another." Frigidity is a huge issue for many couples today, especially early in marriage. I believe frigidity is on the rise because of immorality and premarital sex.

That may sound counterintuitive, since, if you are willing to have sex freely before marriage, surely you will be more sexual in marriage. But I've seen just the opposite.

If you are immoral before marriage, there is actually a good chance you will be frigid in marriage. Why? Before marriage your flesh wants to have its own way by promiscuity and inappropriate sexual activity. So having sex reveals the flesh's desire to take control and rebel against God.

Once in marriage, your flesh wants to have its own way by withholding sex and denying your partner. This is the same self-oriented spirit—the same sin of taking control and rebelling against God. It just reveals itself in opposite behavior.

Paul says to "stop depriving one another except by agreement for a short time," because good sex needs to be a regular part of every marriage. Paul recognizes there is a time and place for withholding sex by mutual agreement, but he says to come back together soon. Why? Because if your mate is not meeting your sexual needs, the devil will find someone who will. Satan knows when there is a sexual problem in a relationship, and he knows how to make the most of it.

That's why we need to guard our marriages tenaciously against adultery. We cannot give the devil a foothold.

Failure in the area of sexuality will completely demolish everything that is precious to you. I watch men and women every year crater over the issue of adultery. They have no idea what they are getting into and never really comprehended the consequences.

The problem for many couples is that everything that leads up to an affair feels so innocent and right. It's a process that Satan tailors to the needs and sensibilities of a man or woman. And everyone is vulnerable.

I took a class in seminary on the home and family living. I can still remember the professor putting the fear of God into us about adultery. He went into morbid detail about everything we would lose if we committed sexual sin—it was like a Scared Straight for pastors. He said that the current statistics meant that more than one of us in the class would one day leave the ministry because of adultery. And not only that; we would be driving off after saying good-bye to our sons and daughters. It was excruciating to consider. I remember one of my classmates leaving the room in tears.

Now, many years later, I know there was at least one man in the class who ended up losing everything because of adultery: the professor.

Proverbs 6:32–33 says,

> The one who commits adultery with a woman is lacking sense;
> He who would destroy himself does it.

Wounds and disgrace he will find,

And his reproach will not be blotted out.

Sex with another woman is not like gossip. Sure they are both sins before God. But this is not a mistake that you can just shake off and have everything go back to the way it was. You can find forgiveness, healing, and restoration, but the consequences of an affair stay with you forever.

I want to expose how an affair happens with six *E* words. This will help protect your marriage in the area of sexuality because an affair will be *E*-asy if you violate them. Protect yourself in these areas, and it will be difficult for Satan to use sex to destroy your marriage.

Elimination

The process of adultery starts when you eliminate the sweetness of romance with your mate. Couples stop doing the little things that show tenderness and endear them to one another. This often happens at three different stages in marriage—during the first year, between years three and seven, and at about year twenty-five.

The first year is a problem for some couples because they are adjusting to the reality of actually being married to and living with this other person. Surprise, surprise—you're married to a real man or woman with real habits and idiosyncrasies. It's not all like those amazing dates you used to have when hormones were raging through your brain.

Years three to seven are a problem for some couples because they have settled into lifestyle patterns and routines that are taking the joy out of their relationship. Their marriage is like a piece of gum that has all the flavor chewed out. They are past the mystery and the myth; now they are down to following the *oughts* and *shoulds* of marriage.

About twenty-five years into marriage is another problem time for many couples. The kids are gone, and the spouses realize they don't really know each other anymore. She looks across the breakfast table and realizes he is not as studly as he was twenty-five years before. He comes home from work and thinks she's not as pretty as she used to be. They've drifted apart over time.

In all these stages, trouble starts when a couple doesn't have a great biblical foundation about the author of marriage, the rules of marriage, the purpose of marriage, and the roles of marriage. A wife stops telling her husband, "[You are] dazzling and ruddy, / Outstanding among ten thousand" (Song of Sol. 5:10). A husband forgets how to, as Song of Solomon says, make his lips drip "with liquid myrrh" and to have hands as "rods of gold" (see 5:13–14). When she stops supplying respect and he stops supplying tenderness, a vital part of their marriage has been eliminated. A vacuum is created. A husband and a wife start looking to fill this vacuum somewhere. That leads to the next step down the path.

Encounter

As I talk with couples, I find a common pattern. After tenderness is eliminated, there is an encounter with a third person. It's usually not about a wife going to a club to meet a Chippendale's dancer or a husband going to a bar to meet a topless dancer.

Instead, it's a normal, everyday encounter. A woman he works with smiles at him one day and says, "It's a delight to work with you." He hasn't had that kind of admiration from a woman in a long time. She is at lunch with friends and a male acquaintance says to her, "I love your smile." Her husband hasn't said that to her for nine years.

So a man whose wife sees sex as a reward that she grudgingly gives him is standing around the copier one day when this woman says, "You are so funny. I love talking to you." A wife who lives with a husband who has an acidic tongue interacts with a man who looks deeply into her eyes and listens to her opinions.

This third party begins to supply the honor hormone. This husband enjoys hanging around this woman because when he is with her, he doesn't feel like a failure—he feels like a real man. He begins to reciprocate and treats her the way she is treating him. It's the way he used to treat his wife.

This wife no longer feels unloved, and she begins to be affectionate and giving toward this man. She says things to him that she has only dreamed of saying to her husband.

When tenderness has been eliminated, Satan will make sure there is an encounter. That's what he did with David and Bathsheba: "Then it happened in the spring, at the time when kings go out to battle, that David sent Joab and his servants with him and all Israel, and they destroyed the sons of Ammon and besieged Rabbah. But David stayed at Jerusalem. Now when evening came David arose from his bed and walked around on the roof of the king's house, and from the roof he saw a woman bathing; and the woman was very beautiful in appearance. So David sent and inquired about the woman. And one said, 'Is this not Bathsheba, the daughter of Eliam, the wife of Uriah the Hittite?'" (2 Sam. 11:1–3).

Enjoyment

Nothing is inherently wrong with having an encounter with a kind third party. In fact, it's impossible to caulk yourself off in marriage so that you never encounter a nice person of the opposite sex. You will always be in situations where you encounter people who are neat and interesting. The problem comes when you let your enjoyment take hold of your senses.

In these encounters, sparks start flying and then fall on your flesh. It's like lighting a sparkler on the Fourth of July. You have to hold it away from your body to keep from burning your arm. These encounters and connections with the opposite sex are the same way. You have to deal with it, and you need to be ready to deal with it long before it happens. That's the only way to have better love now.

I know all about this as a pastor. I'm in the relationship business. Any pastor who tells you that he can spend time with a neat, beautiful, kind, gentle woman—who smiles at him and tells him how much she appreciates him—and not feel deep appreciation and warmth is either lying or dead, or perhaps both.

The day that you don't feel affection for neat people is the day you're not human anymore. But it can't go any further than the Bible allows. Paul tells Timothy to relate to the older men as fathers, the younger men as brothers, the older women as mothers, and the younger women as sisters in all purity. He is saying, "Treat these women as you would a sister."

Men cannot get away from attractive, interesting women. And women can't seal themselves off from nice, good-looking guys. That's why you have to prepare now for the moment when it comes. If you are a husband, there will be a woman that you will to have to keep out of your head. If you are a wife, there will be a day when you have to keep another man out of your head. If you let that spark fall on your flesh and ignite, it will destroy you.

Paul is a great example for us. The greetings he sends in Romans 16 show that he had lots of female friends. He obviously had deep and meaningful interactions with them over a period of months and years, but he stayed pure.

Don't nurture a connection with the other party. Don't extend the conversation by asking an innocent question. Don't walk with them to their car to say good-bye. Don't take some work by their desk to have another chance to say hi. When you do these things, you are building a fantasy island. Soon you'll start daydreaming about how great this relationship is and how fun it is to talk and spend time together. Building this fantasy world puts you in danger of taking the next step.

Expedite

It's easy to blow on the coals and fan the flame of this relationship. When your marriage is not right because you have gotten lazy and complacent, these interactions with a third party do the same thing to your emotions that cocaine does to your body. You become an emotional junkie. When you are with this special other person, it's intoxicating.

You have a married man who is living on the straight and narrow but begins to flirt with this emotion, straying further and further with every encounter. Lust brings an ever-decreasing pleasure but has an ever-increasing desire. So a man starts to flirt a little and spend time with a co-worker in the break room. Then she begins to share personal details that she shouldn't. But it feels good to say deep things and have a man listen to her.

It's the same thing that made you fall in love in the first place. I can still remember where I was sitting in the Black Hawk Café the first time I really bared my soul to Teresa. She listened. She didn't hurt me. It's romantic to be vulnerable and treated with kindness.

When you start substituting this outside relationship for what should be happening in your marriage and start fanning the flames, a few innocuous interactions will never be enough. You'll hand her the papers and let your hands touch. She'll start rationalizing why she is talking to this man and why it feels so good.

At that moment, it takes spiritual discipline to say, "I will go back to my home and make things right instead of just making things different." Every step you take into this new relationship makes it harder and harder to stop.

Years ago a young woman in our church entered into a platonic relationship with another man. She and her husband were leaving town one day, and she began to hyperventilate at the thought of being away from her friend.

At that point it hurts so badly to say no to that new relationship and turn back to one that seems broken. Who wants to have to rekindle what isn't on fire and ignore this raging inferno of a new relationship? The genius of the devil is not to make you do what you know is wrong; it is to make you do what you think is right. And believe me, if you let your marriage grow cold, nothing will feel as right as an emotional connection to a third person.

So now Satan has you swimming around the bait. You've taken steps to expedite a new relationship, but everything is still behind the scenes. That's when the fifth *E* takes hold.

Expression

In my experience, this is a real turning point for couples. If you get to this step, you are in deep trouble. When you speak or write and solidify what has been hinted at and cultivated, you are now building an actual bridge to your fantasy island. When you start talking to this third party about how much you appreciate them and the relationship, it's like being sucked in by a tractor beam or a giant emotional vacuum cleaner.

How does this happen?

You almost never have someone come out and say, "Let's have an affair." Instead, he thinks, *Shall I let her know how I feel?* She wonders, *What if I misread him?* Both of them consider whether they should cross this bridge. So one day he looks at her and says something like, "I sure enjoy spending time with you." He sends it over like a verbal volley. The worst that can happen is that she won't return it, and it will bounce right off the end of the court. No harm, no foul.

Instead, she looks in his eyes and says, "Really?" She hits it back.

So he gains a little more confidence: "Can I share something from my heart?"

"Sure."

Finally he has enough confidence to say the line that he has thought about a thousand times. "You know, I would give anything to have met you ten years ago." He is just mainlining endorphins. At this point they don't feel wicked. He believes he has legitimate pain. She thinks she has a real grievance against her insensitive man.

Once you cross this bridge to your fantasy island, it is very difficult to go back to reality. A sinister trust has developed with this third party. And unless you take extraordinary action, you will finish with the last step.

Experience

Once you have expressed your attraction to this third party, all you need is fifteen minutes, a hotel room, or a spouse gone away, and—*boom!*—you're toast. At this point you are already there.

There will be a girl who makes you feel like a high school sophomore. There will be a guy who makes you feel like you are still on the drill team. You are going to have to walk by faith and say that man shall not live by his palate but by every word that proceeds from the mouth of God. *I will do what is right.*

If you let it go this far, you will live with lifelong reproach. Proverbs 6:23–35 paints a harsh picture of adulterers and how difficult it is to find restoration, even compared to thieves:

For the commandment is a lamp and the teaching is light;
And reproofs for discipline are the way of life
To keep you from the evil woman,
From the smooth tongue of the adulteress.
Do not desire her beauty in your heart,
Nor let her capture you with her eyelids.
For on account of a harlot one is reduced to a loaf of bread,
And an adulteress hunts for the precious life.
Can a man take fire in his bosom
And his clothes not be burned?

Or can a man walk on hot coals
And his feet not be scorched?
So is the one who goes in to his neighbor's wife;
Whoever touches her will not go unpunished.
Men do not despise a thief if he steals
To satisfy himself when he is hungry;
But when he is found, he must repay sevenfold;
He must give all the substance of his house.
The one who commits adultery with a woman is lacking sense;
He who would destroy himself does it.
Wounds and disgrace he will find,
And his reproach will not be blotted out.
For jealousy enrages a man,
And he will not spare in the day of vengeance.
He will not accept any ransom,
Nor will he be satisfied though you give many gifts.

After you have committed adultery, you can never go back to the way your life was before. Your life is completely different. I told my congregation that if I ever fall into an affair, don't let me back into our pulpit.

The ripples that are sent out from this act just go on and on and on. You will have sent an enduring message to your children that you don't have to stick something out if it is too difficult. You will have taught them that God is faithful to a point and his Word is true to a point, unless something feels good. Then you can punt on God and his Word.

How Can You Avoid an Affair?

Here are several keys to helping you avoid an affair:

- Work at the tenderness of your marriage. Husbands, don't zone out on your partner with TV or the Internet. Be passionate and excited about one another. Wives, don't become a classic, fussy old woman you might see at the local cafeteria-style restaurant. The truth is that your relationship can be just as much fun as when you were first dating, if you work at it. And it can actually be more fun because you weren't supposed to have sex when you were dating.
- When you are struggling and facing temptation, be honest with God. God knows your problems. He knows how you feel. He's not surprised that you are being tempted. He will be there for you.
- Get accountability to help along the way. The co-founder of our church helped me through the years. On two different occasions, he told me I needed to watch out because a woman was getting too close. I listened to him, and looking back, I'm glad I did in both cases.
- Flee. Run away from these situations before they get started. The biggest problems in Christian marriages come from relationships that start out with godly interactions. They are innocent encounters between two sincere Christians, but then they become something more. Run away before they can.
- Have good sex. Especially for men, having good sex pretty much takes the excitement out of the thought of an affair. Most men are not looking for a bikini model and exotic

love-making; they just want to have passionate and fulfilling sex. Make this a regular part of your marriage, and you will go a long way toward preventing an affair.

Sex is powerful. We'll look at how to make it better in the next chapter. But I wanted to remind you to keep it in the right place first. Women, guard your hearts. Men, watch your eyes. Nip things in the bud and keep your marriage bed pure and holy before the Lord. Without that, you definitely won't have better love now.

Chapter 12

What Your Spouse Expects Concerning Sex

PERHAPS NO AREA OF marriage has more baggage and expectations than sex. Guys think about it a lot before they are married (and after as well). Women dream of the romantic tenderness they will one day experience. Then the wedding day arrives, and the reality inevitably can't live up to the hype.

This chapter will help you talk about some of those expectations and ways to help your reality become more of what God wants it to be.

What did your wife expect about sex when she heard you say, "I do"?

A Wife Expects Tenderness

First Peter 3:7 is a classic explanation of how a man should treat his wife: "You husbands in the same way, live with your wives as unto knowledge," as the Greek text says (NASB: "in an understanding way"). We think of Peter as being kind of a rough cob sometimes, and he probably was. But he had divine wisdom when it comes to living with our wife. He says, "Don't be stupid; live as unto knowledge."

And then he goes on to define what "unto knowledge" means—that this woman is not a soft boy. She's not a hairless man. She's a woman. He says, "Live with her as unto knowledge as a weaker vessel." The idea of "weaker" conveys the meaning of china or porcelain or crystal. He's not saying your wife is inferior. A man is made out of lead and pewter, and a woman is made out of porcelain. And everybody knows you handle porcelain gently. A man should be tender with his wife and grant "her honor as a fellow heir of the grace of life."

When a woman hears a man say, "I do," at the altar, she wants a husband who will be tender to her. She wants someone who says, "You're a weaker vessel; you're delicate. There's a difference in how I should talk to you. There's a difference in how I listen to you. There's a difference in my tone of voice when I speak to you."

I have learned this from personal experience. I could give you horror stories. Early in our marriage, I can remember my wife saying to me, "If I wanted to be talked to like that, I would have remained single." She hit me where it hurt, but I probably deserved it.

At least I come by my insensitivity naturally. I grew up in a family of four boys. My father worked as a bomb maker at the A. O. Smith bomb factory. I grew up as an athlete, playing any sport all the time. I also have two sons. One is an athlete; the other shoots people in the head as a federal agent.

So my background helps shape my insensitivity. I have all kinds of stupid male responses to people. I remember one time when Teresa had tears glistening in her eyes, and her was lip quivering. I said, "What's the matter, sweetheart? I saw you dropped your purse, and I kicked it back over to you. What's the problem, honey?"

There are some verses in Proverbs that hit me hard as a man. One goes like this: "There is one who speaks rashly like the thrusts of a sword" (Prov. 12:18). Have you ever done that—said something to your wife and then wished you could take it back? Just like you can't take back a good swing with a sword, so you can't take back stupid words once they've come out of your mouth.

Here's another verse: "A brother offended is harder to be won than a strong city" (Prov. 18:19). Men who can't control their tongues leave a trail of broken relationships that are difficult to mend. That verse goes on to say that "contentions are like the bars of a citadel." When you hurt your spouse with your words, you may say, "Well, I got that out of my system. Now I feel better." But you're fooling yourself. What you've just done is put both of you behind the bars of a prison. Your relationship can't be right until you work it out.

When two men "go off" on each other, they finish and say, "OK, we're through with that. We're good." That's how it works with the guys down at the gym. But when you go off on your wife, she is pulling shrapnel out of herself for about six weeks. We don't understand why she has a problem; we were "just being honest."

About twenty years ago I was at my twentieth high school reunion, hanging out with a group of my old buddies. One of my friends was standing there with his wife who was obviously a gentle, tender, "all-girl" kind of woman. As he was talking, she was trying to put her glasses on but dropped them, picked them up, then dropped them again. Right in the middle of all of us, he stopped what he was saying and said to her, "If you drop them again, I'm going to break them!"

Imagine I took him aside and said, "What in the world are you doing?" He would have been embarrassed and apologetic. He just didn't think about the impact his words would have on his wife.

You just have to learn to treat a woman with tenderness. There's a good reason why God took Eve from Adam's side, from his body. Deep down, everyone wants to take care of their own body. Your body means something to you. And so, God didn't make Eve from the dirt because Adam would have had an excuse to treat her like that. God made Eve from Adam's side.

Jewish tradition says God didn't make her from Adam's feet to be under him or his head to be over him, but from his side so he could draw her close to him. Touch your wife with tenderness; speak to her from a gentle heart.

A woman is often attracted to a man's strength and toughness . . . until she marries him. Unfortunately, some of these men don't know how to turn off their toughness.

Tom Landry was a great player for the New York Giants and a tremendous coach for the Dallas Cowboys. He was a big man, about six foot one and 200 pounds. He was imposing and successful at everything he touched. In high school he was an all-state athlete. Then he flew about thirty bombing missions over Germany and was a decorated soldier. He came back and played for the University of Texas. Then he went to the NFL and played for the New York Giants where he was an All-Pro defensive back. Then he coached the New York Giants to a championship. Finally, he became the first head coach of the Dallas Cowboys and won two Super Bowls.

Tom Landry became a Christian in the 1950s because all of his success was empty. He could find no happiness in his achievements. Even though he was the best at almost every stage of his life, he could not find meaning. But he found that meaning through Christ, and his Christianity influenced every area of his life.

On top of everything else, Tom Landry was a great husband to his wife, Alicia, and faithful to her until the day he died. At training camp every summer, she would come out to the field at the end of the day. Tom would get an Eskimo Pie then hold Alicia's hand while they walked off the Dallas Cowboys' practice field. He'd put his arm around her and hold her close to him. He'd take her to the cafeteria and pull out her chair for her. He knew how to turn off the testosterone and be tender with his wife.

I once counseled a man who had busted one marriage and was about to ruin another one. I asked his wife, "When do you think your problems started in your marriage?"

He interrupted, "October 12, 1978, which is the day we got married."

I turned to his wife and asked, "How do you feel right now?"

She couldn't even say a complete sentence. "Murderous. Condescended to. Insulted. Hurt. Alienated."

I said to this genius of a man, "If you will say something like that in a counseling office, what kinds of things do you say in your own house?" This was a man who didn't care that he was an oaf; he didn't learn to be tender with his wife.

For a woman, sex cannot be separated from tenderness. It is an act of supreme vulnerability on her part, as she willingly accepts and receives her husband. Men, if you want good sex, create an atmosphere of tenderness that pervades your relationship.

I realize that men who are reading this are probably saying, "Wow, what a great way to end this book! When is he going to start insulting my mother?" Just remember, you'll get your turn when we deal with what a man thought about sex when he heard his wife say, "I do."

A Wife Expects Romance

Every woman who has ever stood at the altar and said, "I do," expected her marriage would contain *romance*. Romance is the visceral aspect of love. It's not just devotion until death. It's not just spiritual leadership. It's not just sexuality. Romance is carefully communicating from the heart how you love somebody. The term *romance* comes from the Middle Ages when Latin was the formal language. But in areas of the heart—stories, songs, tales—you didn't speak in Latin, you spoke the vernacular, *romance*. Romance was the vernacular language of France. It was the language of the heart. By the seventeenth century, the word *romance* connoted displays of heartfelt affection.

Imagine you are at a restaurant for dinner. You see a couple enter. The man holds the door for the woman. He puts his arm around her shoulder as they walk to their table. He pulls out her chair for her. He looks into her eyes as they are talking. At one point you see him reach across and tenderly take her hand. What's your first thought? *That couple is obviously not married.* Sad, but true.

See, marriage is not a "let's make a covenant until death, to have kids, see who dies first, and see who gets the insurance out of this" thing. That's not why you got married.

Nobody marries for pragmatic reasons. Have you seen a woman look at a man and say, "Now there's a good mechanic; he'd be handy to have around the house"? Or "Let me see your teeth there. Not bad." How many men do you know who've said, "Now there's a woman that can do a load of wash"? Every couple I've ever met can trace their relationship back to a restaurant, to a park bench, to a dance, to some time and place when their souls connected.

Romance is when somebody gets inside of you and touches you, and you say, "I need about a half century of this." Of course, the problem is that before marriage we do romance as a means to procure our mate. After the wedding, romance has to become a discipline. You have to stop and say, "I'm going to be tender, I'm going to go the extra mile to make my spouse feel special, I'm going to be gentle, I'm going to be giving."

I love my cell phone. It's great for romance. I can just call home at anytime and say, "Hey, baby, I was thinking of you. I'm out; is there anything I can get for you?" I do that just to let her know I care about her. Men, it's a conscious decision you make to pay attention to your wife and provide romance.

I told one restaurant story, so here's the opposite. My wife and I went out to eat, and I saw a woman come in and sit down. I looked down and saw the ring; she was married and probably waiting for her husband. She was dressed really nice. She looked pretty. She had spent some time on herself.

A few minutes later I watched a man come in and sit down with her. You could tell he had put in his eight to ten hours at work. He was tired. She turned to face him and talked, and he just stared ahead. He ate his quesadillas like his arm was on a hinge. She would say something to him. He would just stare at his plate or look over her shoulder.

Have you ever played tennis by yourself? You can hit the ball over the net and watch it bounce until it hits the back fence. If you've ever done that, you probably didn't do it for very long. It's not very exciting to hit the ball and watch it bounce against a fence. You're going to quit.

So I watched this man at the restaurant (while paying attention to my own wife). I wanted to go over there and grab him and say, "Hey, Bozo! This woman is hurting. She wants you to talk. Just look at her and say hi to her."

The sad thing is this marriage is being set up. I know Satan is going to find somebody who will talk to her. She was an attractive lady who just wanted her husband to think about her for a few minutes. Eventually she turned straight ahead, and they sat in silence to finish their dinners. She felt like a loser and an idiot for trying so hard.

I guarantee you she lay in bed that night with dreams of what it could have been like. All her husband had to do was just be nice. He didn't have to be Cary Grant—just courteous, just nice, just talk to her, touch her hand. Just interrupt her to say, "You are so pretty; thank you for all that you do." That's all he had to do, but he didn't, and she went away hurt. Men, how often could that be your wife?

A woman needs to know from a man's heart, "I love you and I appreciate you." She needs to feel that a man is intentionally creating an environment of romance in their relationship. Romance leads to good sex and to better love now.

A Wife Expects Sex

Another thing a woman expected when she heard, "I do," is good old-fashioned sex. Ten years ago I wouldn't have included this on the list. However, for the last six or seven years I've been doing Song of Solomon conferences in key churches around the country. There may be two or three thousand people in attendance at one of these events. And at almost every one there is at least one woman who comes up to me and says, "What if you really like exciting sex, but your husband just doesn't have any kind of drive?" The first time a woman came and said that to me, I couldn't stop myself before I said, "Really?"

One of the earliest times this happened was at a conference in the deep South. A man came up to me during a break and said, "Brother Tommy, what if one of you has sexual desires that are a little bit more risqué than the other one?"

I stopped him and gave him my stock answer, "Brother, you've got to be patient with your wife; you can't be asking her to do something she's not willing to do."

He looked shocked and said, "Oh, no, it's not me, it's her! She likes a lot of crazy things."

I told him, "Friend, that's what you call an answered prayer." I used my most compassionate counseling voice and said, "Idiot, get back in there, shut up, and enjoy yourself."

Consider 1 Corinthians 7:3–4: "The husband must fulfill his duty to his wife . . . the husband does not have authority over his own body, but the wife does." I used to read that and think, "What a waste of scroll and ink!" Never in my life have I ever had to say to my wife, "No, no, no!" while she is chasing me around the kitchen table, yelling, "Yes, I'll have you now!"

I have a hard time imagining any man who, during the pleasure of sex, would open his Bible and say, "Can this be of God?" He already knows the answer. But the reality is that many women are unfulfilled sexually in their marriages. For many women, there comes a time in their lives where it becomes an act of obedience.

A wife needs sex in the way that a woman understands sex. It should be tender—an expression of masculine love. To quote from that classic fount of wisdom, the movie *City Slickers,* "A woman needs a reason, a man needs a place." You have to learn signals from each other. You just don't say, "Yo, sex, ten o'clock, be there!" You listen to each other's hearts. You have to be sensitive to certain things she says or does. A husband needs to tenderly express his physical love for his wife in a way that she wants to receive.

If you haven't noticed, sex is rigged. The deck is stacked by God. Men and women are different, so that both of them get stretched in the area of sexuality.

Imagine if women had men's sex drives. Wouldn't that be great? The problem is that we'd be like little rabbits all the time. And sex would just feed your lust. God wasn't going to let it happen that way. Imagine if men had women's sex drive. Marriage would be this incredible, long conversation. You could talk for days; you'd forget to eat. Instead, God rigged sex so that sometimes a woman has to consciously decide, "I'm going to give myself to this man." And a man has to say, "You know, I'm going to slow down a little bit and talk to her and hold her."

As your character gets stretched by the complexities of your sexual relationship, sex becomes an act of holiness. It becomes more than just an act of hormones and passion. If sexuality in marriage were nothing but passion, what city in the United States would have the greatest marriages? Hollywood. It has the best-looking men and women. They have the best bodies. They certainly focus on sex. So if it were all about lust and passion, their marriages would be great.

But instead the marriages in Hollywood are the fodder for late-night comedy routines. Their marriages are bad because their lives are centered on themselves. They are takers. They are not givers.

Marriage is a rigged institution. Only the holy survive. Marriage is varsity ball. The ante goes up when you allow someone to invade your personal space. You don't get to play games and put on masks with your mate. This person is in your face all the time. And if you don't walk by the standard of Christ, you're in trouble. If you try to just get by, you will eventually find yourself in a big mess. Only the standard of Christ is high enough to see you through. If you want to live a selfish life, marriage is a pretty unfair institution. But God made it ruthlessly perfect for helping us learn to lay down our lives for Christ and our mates. Men, give your wives sex in the way they want to receive it. That's the only way to get better love now when it comes to sex.

Men also have expectations when it comes to sex. That's not a big surprise. In general, men think about sex a lot more than women do. And for a man, sex touches something very central to who he is and what he believes about himself.

A Husband Expects Fulfilling Sex

Most people think that when a man got married, he expected sex. That's actually an incorrect statement propagated by our culture. It's not that a man needs sex—what a man needs is *fulfilling sex.*

There's a big difference. I had a man say to me one time, "You know, whenever I make love to my wife, I feel like I'm a bee circling an inert flower to pollinate it. There is no response in her whatsoever." A man doesn't want a wife who is just being a good Christian martyr. They used to tell girls in England on their honeymoon to lie there and think of England—"Endure it for the sake of the country." No man wants to have sex with a woman who is quoting her favorite Scriptures—"I can do all things through Christ who strengthens me" and "Yea, though I walk through the valley of the shadow of death . . ."

If you ask a woman how to have good sex, she will say it involves a man who is tender and gentle and cares for her. If you ask a man, he will talk about a woman who is responsive to him, is creative, and is exciting. That's what he's thinking.

Part of Titus 2:4 says, "encourage the young women to love their husbands." Some of you may be thinking, *I wish I had heard this when I was nineteen.* That's why you need to take this stuff to the next generation because you need to learn this when you're coming out of college and preparing for marriage.

One of the ladies in our church is in charge of our weddings, and she noticed that many of the young brides had questions about sex that they could never ask their mothers. Now she does a class for about three girls at a time. They look at the real issues that confront them sexually in marriage. Somebody has to teach them these things.

And this is biblical. I cover this in more detail in my book, *The Book of Romance*, but the Bible is a very sensual book. Consider one text from chapter 7 of the Song of Solomon. The man in this chapter starts at the bottom of his wife's feet and goes to the top of her head, talking about how exciting she is to him. He talks about her looks, her character, her beauty, and his respect for her.

She is absolutely thrilling to him. In verse 8, the man says, "I will climb the palm tree." He speaks of his wife as an oasis, as a palm tree. And he says, "I will climb the palm tree, I will take hold of its fruit stalks." Now that's a great verse. He's going to go up his wife and enjoy her. Verse 8 also says, "Oh, may your breasts be like clusters of the vine, and the fragrance of your breath like apples." Now that's a verse you've never seen on the sign outside of a church. In verse 9, he says, "And your mouth [is] like the best wine!"

Overall the picture is that he is pretty much going to devour this woman. And that's straight from the Bible.

In the second half of verse 9, we believe the woman continues the thought for the husband. (If you're married, I'm sure that's never happened to you. Actually, I say to my wife sometimes, "Make up my mind!") After he says her mouth is like wine, she's like apples, and her breasts are like the clusters, she says, "It goes down smoothly." She's saying that, yes, she is like wine and she goes down smooth.

One time I asked my wife, "What do you think is the gender sin of women?"

She said, "We get fussy."

"What about men?"

"Men's problem is they get shallow emotionally. You guys will just kind of go to the bank, make withdrawals, and want to have sex, but without taking the time to nurture us."

That's why in the first nine verses the man is nurturing this woman; he creates a heart in this woman that can ignite. My wife said that "we women tend to get fussy; we get to be old biddies." You know how it is—something exciting is about to happen and the woman says, "Stop it, stop it, stop it. Remember your triglycerides."

This woman is not like that; she says, "It goes down smoothly." She is not resistant or disinterested. A man can be turned away by his wife only so many times. If a woman continually keeps her husband at arm's length or acts like she is doing him a favor, it's debilitating. That man doesn't like continually feeling like a loser, so after a while, he says, "Just forget it. I'm not going to be humiliated anymore."

In the Song of Solomon, their love is like wine, "flowing gently through the lips of those who fall asleep" (v. 9). The idea is that the man has enjoyed her and drunk deeply of her. They are drunk on each other's love, spent and exhausted, and they fall asleep in each other's arms. I recommend it. This is a great memory verse.

Everybody always thinks the Bible is against sex. Let me tell you, on your raciest day, you will never touch this book. The Song of Solomon is to sexuality and passion what Romans is to the righteousness of God. The woman is responsive to the man. And in verse 10, she brags about it: "I am my beloved's, / And his desire is for me." That word *desire* is the word for consuming something. She's proud that this man wants to consume her and that no other woman can meet his need.

But not only is she responsive; she's also aggressive. In verse 11, she says, "Come, my beloved, let us go into the country. / Let us spend the night in the villages." Did you know it's OK to spend the night in a hotel even after you're married? It's OK. Hotels aren't just for your honeymoon. This woman is saying to her husband, "Meet me outside of town at the Sheraton and come rested." When I teach this material at conferences, it's at about this point that the men are saying, "Yeah, this guy's great. I like him. God's hand is on this man."

The wife goes on in verse 12 and compares their love to a vineyard. "Let us see whether the vine has budded / And its blossoms have opened, / And whether the pomegranates have bloomed." She's saying that she wants to see if the delight of their romance has ended. Too many couples would have to say that the vineyard is dead. "That's something we did way back in the 1980s, all right, but don't you think we are a little past that?" But this woman in Song of Solomon is going to take her man away and show him that the vineyard is alive and well.

The root of a mandrake plant is shaped like a man's body. In those days, they believed if the woman ate mandrakes, it would increase her libido and her ability to bear children. So in the book of Genesis Leah and Rachel quarreled over who would give mandrakes to Jacob. It's sending a strong signal to a man. "Don't the mandrakes smell good? Would you like one?" It's the same thing today as a woman saying, "Meet me at the Fairfield Inn and bring some Viagra."

In the Song of Solomon, she says, "I have fruits for you—fruits new, and fruits old." There are old ways that we touch each other, and we know what they're like. But she also says, "I have new things for you. I have delights for you that you have never experienced before, and I have saved them up for you."

This is why someone in the church needs to talk to young men and to young women. We had a couple in our church named Carl and Carol. Carol had a real ministry to young women. Whenever she went on women's retreats, the young women would inevitably congregate with her in her hotel room. She was wonderful at talking with them about biblical sexuality and how to please a man. Sometimes she'd end up with fifteen or twenty wide-eyed listeners in her hotel room.

After a few years, when it was time for women to sign up for the retreat, their husbands would stop me and ask, "Brother Tommy, will Carol be on this retreat? If so, I'll do whatever I have to do." When Carl and Carol moved to another city, the men in our church wore black for weeks.

A woman needs to study the art of delighting her husband. It's also important to say that a man can make it easier for a woman to do this. When a man is not kind and gentle, it is the most unmotivating thing in the world for a woman. She feels like she's reinforcing bad behavior in her husband. "I don't want to give him the notion that I like what he's doing." When a man is unkind to his wife, her light goes out. A woman's body is connected to her soul. Cherish and nurture to keep the flame alive. So, guys, if you want a Song of Solomon wife, you need to be a Song of Solomon husband. That starts with cherishing your wife from the bottom of her feet to the top of her head. Tell her about her character, her beauty, and your love for her. And back up your talk with action in terms of being kind, considerate, and gentle. Then she won't feel like she's giving self-destructive affirmation to a godless husband. A man's role is to nurture and cherish his wife; a woman's role is to respond to him.

Every wife ought to reach Proverbs 7 to see how a harlot gets inside a man's head. I read an article one time (you won't read an illustration like this in many of your Christian books) that interviewed a prostitute on what it took to be successful. I was amazed at what she said. She said, "The myth is that a hooker is a temptress. The reality is that you need the ability to provide what that man's wife forgot. You have to remember the art of being a woman." That may be the worst illustration you'll ever read, but it's true. Isn't it sad that a prostitute would understand what too many wives forget?

When a man said, "I do," he expected that his wife would be exciting and responsive to him. A man needs fulfilling sex.

Sex is such an important part of marriage. You both have to communicate and work together to make sure this fence post stays strong. If this one starts to rot on the inside, it will break off in ways that have disastrous consequences for years to come. You don't want to go there. Help each other have good sex, so that you can have better love now.

Keeping the Fence Post Solid

Key Concepts about Sex

- Sex is a physical demonstration of your spiritual union with your spouse.
- Failure in the area of sexuality will demolish everything that is precious to you.
- Be careful that tenderness doesn't get eliminated from your marriage.
- Avoid relationships with third parties where they supply tenderness and respect.
- For a wife, sex cannot be separated from tenderness, respect, and romance.
- A husband expects passionate, fulfilling sex.

Straightening the Post

Discussion for Better Love Now

1. What are some of the attitudes in our culture today toward sex? How have you been influenced by these attitudes?

2. Why do you think sex is so powerful for men? What about for women?

3. As a wife, how do you feel about the tenderness, respect, and romance in your marriage? What is a concrete step you both could take to make sex more meaningful for you?

4. As a husband, would you say your marriage has passionate, fulfilling sex? What is a concrete step you both could take to make sex more meaningful for you?

Conclusion

NAMING A BOOK IS an interesting process. You'd be surprised how many titles get tried and discarded before you finally hit on the right one. One of the runners up for this book was *What Your Mate Thought You Meant When You Said, "I Do."* It seemed to fit because men and women have totally different ideas, notions, expectations, and disappointments in the areas of love and marriage.

Any marriage that works takes these differences into account. Good marriages are good because the differences are understood and accommodated. Bad marriages are bad due to ignorance of these differences or the downright refusal to serve a spouse.

These differences are actually a gift from God. Can you imagine what marriage would be like if God made us the same in our makeup? Marriage would become simply a vehicle to gratify ourselves through somebody who was just like us. It would become the ultimate venue for selfishness.

But God didn't do it that way. He rigged marriage. To be proper and delightful spouses, we have to deny ourselves and serve. We cannot simply follow our own instincts and lusts. Marriage demands an entry fee—piety. Seeking another's good is the ante to get in the game. Marriage is not Little League; you're playing with the big boys now. Selfish and rebellious people are going to always struggle in this divine arrangement.

In the book of Genesis, we see both the origins of man and the origins of marriage. Adam knows God before Adam receives Eve. Eve sees God her Creator before she sees Adam. We were made to first relate to God and honor his Word before relating to each other.

My guess is that when you picture the perfect spouse, you are picturing someone who is selfless, loving, and servant oriented. The problem is that none of those people exist in nature. You can only find qualities like that in God and in those who fear him. You are really looking for someone who is godly, Christlike, spiritual, and holy. You may not hear these terms a lot in the marketplace today, but they are lovely beyond measure when they describe a husband or a wife.

Since we are different, the coin of the realm in marriage is wisdom, patience, understanding, selflessness, and love. All the vows of a wedding, all the grandeur of a ceremony, all the beauties of a bride, and all the thrills of a honeymoon will not help a marriage that has lost its heart. To enjoy marriage as it was meant to be, you have to be who you were meant to be. Spend time with Christ in his Word, submit to your church, and walk in God's enabling grace. Even with this, the differences between a man and a woman will try you, test you, humble you, and refine you. And it will be outstanding.

Rightly did Martin Luther say, "Marriage did for me what no monastery could."

Happy trails!

Appendix

Living as a Mother- or Father-in-Law

SOME OF THE FOLKS reading this book will be dealing with an empty nest and grown children. The complexities of family relationships in marriage don't end when your children leave the home. As a matter of fact, when those children get married, you have entered into one of the most challenging relationships of your life.

I'm going to speak in a few generalities here, but I think this will be useful for you to consider. In my experience, the most difficult of the relationship hindrances comes from the man's mother.

When I do weddings, I can't help but watch the mother of the bride and the mother of the groom. I've stood at altars and watched them for thirty years. The bride's mother is the coach of the wedding. She watches her daughter walking and thinks, *Get your bouquet up! Bring it up! Slow down!* She is entering a new phase with her daughter: coaching.

The groom's mother, on the other hand, hasn't been fixing a beautiful dress on her daughter. She hasn't been making sure the veil sits just right on her head. No, she's sitting there quietly, thinking about how this bride is about to step between her and her son. And when the bride and groom stare into each other's eyes, you can just see her go under.

The other relationship that seems to struggle is between the girl and her father because there's a man that's about to take his baby. I have known men who would regularly send large stipends and bags of new clothes to their daughters, so that they would be taken care of. That becomes intrusive real quick.

For whatever reason, the bride's mother seems to be less of an issue, and the guy's father is usually the most laid back. He's laughing. You'll see him out in the parking lot, telling his buddies, "He's her problem now—what goes around comes around."

I'll say, "Sir, would you like me to pray for your son?"

"Naw, pray for his wife."

Whatever your life situation, if you are an in-law here are seven rules that can help you maximize the impact of your new relationships:

1. Don't Criticize

Don't say something negative about your son's wife or your daughter's husband. Don't even insinuate it. "My, my, son, you're looking thin. Are you being fed?" "Is this house hygienic? No wonder you've been sick so much lately." Don't say that. Whenever you criticize your child's spouse, you force your child to defend his mate to his momma or daddy. That is a very difficult spot to be in. They have to choose between being disloyal to you or to their spouse. So don't criticize.

2. Be Sensitive with Suggestions

There are times when you can and should take your child aside to offer to help them. But be careful that you only take as much ground as you are given. Young people often want to fly on their own, just like most of us did when we were their age.

Don't be trigger-happy with advice because you see fifteen things they can do differently. God took care of you; he'll take care of them. So pick your battles. Just after my son got married, I had lunch with one of the leading evangelical preachers in the world. After he heard I had become an in-law, he leaned forward and said, "Let me give you some advice: don't try to jump in there and help your kid too much. I was well-meaning, but I alienated a couple of my kids." Be sensitive to saying as much as your child is willing to hear.

3. Don't Show Up Unannounced

Privacy is a precious thing. Call before you come over to your children's house—especially if you are the man's parents. I went through these ideas with my wife, and she said, "If my parents show up at our house and the place is a mess, it's OK because they know me. But your parents are still under the illusion that I'm a great housekeeper. I need some warning so that I can at least mitigate the disaster." So, if you're his parents, make sure to call and ask before coming over.

4. Let Them Struggle

We have the tendency to want to rescue our children. Don't do it. God uses adversity to help us learn lessons that we couldn't otherwise learn. Let your kids struggle, or you will rob them of these valuable lessons. There are obviously situations that get so bad that you need to lend a hand, but you need to let your children handle their routine crises on their own.

5. Don't Give Money That Isn't Asked For

Quite often, money is a means of control. Proverbs 23:1–7 says that when you sit down to eat with a rich man, it's like putting a knife to your throat because his delicacies are false and you may vomit them up. In other words, the rich man is not giving; he's buying. He's controlling you from his wealth.

Make sure that you give money only after you and your children have talked about it. Teresa and I married before she had finished college. Her dad said to me, "I've put Teresa through college all of these years. Would you allow me to keep paying for her college?" I tried to act like I was actually thinking about it, then blurted out, "Yes!" as fast as I could.

But what if money had just kept showing up over the next few years with a note attached, saying, "This isn't for you, Tommy. This is for Teresa"? That's a whole different ball game. I would have felt threatened. But my father-in-law was gracious enough to go through the newly established chain of command. He came through me. And I said, "Sure."

A few years later, my father-in-law was breaking up his oil company and dividing the assets among his five children. He came to me and said, "Would you allow me to give you all some money as we break up a percentage of this oil company?" At the time, we had just started our church, and so we were pulling down about $400 a month. He knew that I would take the money. But he didn't just show up with a check because that would have made me his servant.

Instead, he served me and asked me. Here was this extremely gifted, successful man—one of the five greatest men I've ever known—who came and asked my permission because he recognized the divinity of the role that I'd stepped into as a husband. That's a smart man.

6. Don't Divide the Couple

Don't send money and say, "Son, this is for you to use on whatever you'd like." That's the same thing as saying that this is for you and not your wife. You can't do that. You should not direct money or gifts. If there's a specific need that you've talked about that affects one spouse more than the other, and it's agreed to, then that's fine. But don't try to control your child by giving money. Treat them as what they are: one flesh. You can't just treat your son or daughter. They are a couple now.

7. Don't Obligate Your Child

Many parents exert passive control to get their own way. "Well, Christmas is coming in a few weeks. Our house is so wonderful at holidays when it is filled with family." *Nudge, nudge.* Maybe they want you to spend Christmas with them.

I love driving down to my wife's folks' place at Christmas. We've done it now for almost thirty years. And we go down to see my mother. But we go because we want to, not because we are expected to. And there was no pressure put on me.

Don't manipulate or obligate your kids. Don't say, "We signed over our house to you, so that when your father and I pass away, this can be your home." Perhaps they don't want to live in your house. Don't send a check to your daughter and say, "You've always wanted to start a master's program. We're giving you the money to start." If you talked about that and they both agreed to it, you can. But don't do it to make your daughter start the program because now you're going around her husband.

These problems first arise at weddings. Man, have we had some interesting scenes at weddings in our church—scenes by the bride, scenes by the groom, but mostly scenes from the parents. On one occasion, our marriage coordinator said, "We should ban all parents from these weddings." One mother made such a morose demonstration of her grief in "losing" her son to the bride that she had to be practically carried down the aisle, weeping. She cried during the wedding. Finally a friend told her in a stage whisper, "You're disgracing God and your child. Shut up!"

A wedding is basically a bride's show. Have you ever seen a magazine called *Grooms*? Have you ever seen little seven-year-old boys outside playing wedding? Marching in their pretend tuxedos? No, it's the bride who gets the wedding. (Honeymoons are for grooms.)

If you ask young girls what kind of wedding they would like, most of them can tell you in some detail. Ask a young man the same question some day: "What kind of wedding have you dreamed of?"

"You're supposed to think about them beforehand?" he replies. "I know you're supposed to have a ring or something."

Men don't think about weddings. And so, when your daughter gets married, assist your daughter in enjoying her wedding—just like you wanted your mother to do when you got married. You didn't want your mother to use you to make a social statement in your community. So don't you do it with your daughter. Let her get married the way she wants to get married. Of course you have the right to say, "I can't afford this." "No, we can't fly John Mayer in for the reception, dear."

I have seen weddings where a possessive mother made her daughter just want to get the wedding over with at any cost. The bride and the groom can't enjoy it; they are just trying to limit the damage. Let your daughter have the wedding she wants, and if she asks your opinion, give your opinion. Be there to help her.

Colossians 3 says, "Let the peace of Christ rule in your hearts." Let Christ always be the peacemaker. He's the Prince of Peace.

As in-laws, be a source of blessing and strength for your child's new family. My life was made better in so many ways when I married into my wife's family. I inherited Teresa's parents and two brothers and two sisters, and it has been a delight. They have been an encouragement and a blessing.

Are you and your spouse on the same page about your relationship to your grown children? If not, it will not only undermine your relationship with your children but will also undermine your relationship with one another. So many couples who have been married for twenty-five or thirty years have a simmering conflict because they never agreed on how to relate to their grown children.

Get this settled between the two of you and be a blessing to your kids. Being in-laws who honor God and his Word will help you both have better love now.

Notes

1. Bureau of the Census, U.S. Department of Commerce,"Measuring 50 years of economic change," http://www.census.gov/prod/3/98pubs/p60-203.pdf.

2. Lina Guzman, "Effects of Wives' Employment on Marital Quality," NSFH Working Paper no. 85, http://www.ssc.wisc.edu/cde/nsfhwp/nsfh85.pdf.

3. John M. Gottman, PhD, and Nan Silver, *The Seven Principles for Making Marriage Work* (New York: Three Rivers Press, 1999).

4. I discussed these only briefly in my book *12 Essentials of Godly Success*, but I want to go into more detail here about how to apply them to your marriage.

5. Stephen Ross, "Charles Thomas Studd," Worldwide Missions Missionary Biographies, http://www.wholesomewords.org/missions/biostudd.html (accessed November 19, 2005).

A Special Note from Tommy

A WORD OF THANKS NEEDS to be given to all who prayed for me this last year. I fell into a clinical depression in June 2006 and found myself in that black hole of joylessness and anxiety that accompanies it. Never have the words "I'll pray for you" meant so much. I also came to realize the real nature of "for better or for worse." I said to my wife so many times, "I'm sorry, honey; you never signed on for this." Teresa merely responded with, "I signed on for you and whatever comes with you." I found out that a great many marriages break up when a depression sets in because the mates usually have no earthly idea what their mates are going through. Teresa was continually there for me with strength, poise, and counsel. It brought a closeness through the fire that we had never known. A number of wonderful things resulted from the depression, but one of them was a deeper respect and appreciation of the woman who followed through on her vow made thirty-two years earlier when she did not even know what "depression" was. Our vows are made with such a glibness and sense of rote and tradition, but when marriage moves from the chapel into the face of reality, all the dross is burned away and only the harsh truth of character is left. Praise God for a yokefellow who stayed straight in the yoke in difficult plowing.